The
Survival Guide
for Working Moms
(and Other Stressed-Out Adults)

Diana Zuckerman, Ph.D.
Brandel France de Bravo, M.P.H.
National Research Center for Women & Families

Illustrated by
Tina Druce-Hoffman

www.quill.com

Published by Quill Corporation, Lincolnshire, IL
www.quill.com

Printed in the United States of America

First Edition

Special thanks to Christy Wolf, editor

CONTENTS

Letter from Quill's President V

Introduction. VII

Chapter 1. **Organizing My Home and Life** 1

Chapter 2. **Reducing Stress for a Healthier
You and a Healthier Family** 7

Chapter 3. **Rise and Shine: Getting Enough Sleep** 13

Chapter 4. **Choosing the Right Child Care** 21

Chapter 5. **How Can I Teach My Kids to Behave?** 31

Chapter 6. **Healthy Eating for Families** 41

Chapter 7. **Kids, TV, and Video Games** 49

Chapter 8. **Tips to Keep You and Your
Family Healthy** 57

Chapter 9. **Back to School: Getting off on the
Right Foot** 69

Chapter 10. **Kids and the Internet** 79

Chapter 11. **Finding Time for Yourself (and Your
Special Other) in a Hectic World** 89

Chapter 12. **Caring for an Aging Parent** 97

Chapter 13. **The Single Parent—Riding a
Bicycle Built for Two...Alone** 111

Chapter 14. **Plan B: What to Do in an
Emergency or When Things
Don't Go As Planned** 119

Chapter 15. **Help for the Holidays** 129

LETTER FROM QUILL'S PRESIDENT

One of my strongest beliefs is that family always comes first. Work comes second.

That being said, we do count on our jobs for the money we need to pay our bills, so I think what's really important is to achieve the right balance between family and work. I know creating this balance isn't always easy—meetings run late, emails and phone calls need to be returned, and every new work project seems to be "hot"—but I truly believe that a well-rounded, well-rested individual who has their priorities straight is ultimately more productive at work and a whole lot happier in life.

Since the standard 9-to-5 job is now a thing of the past for most of us working folks, I think our challenge today is to make the most of our time away from work, no matter how limited that time may be. For me, it's spending time with my wife and kids, watching my favorite Boston sports teams play on TV, and finding time to exercise every day to clear my head and help sweat away the stress.

Whatever you do to make the most of your family time, I think you'll find the information in this book very useful. We tried to cover everything that's important to the millions of people—just like you—who juggle work and family responsibilities, so you'll see a wide range of issues addressed: staying organized, reducing stress, getting more sleep, raising your kids and much, much more.

I do want to say that this book isn't meant to be the definitive source for "perfect" solutions (after all, every family is thankfully unique, and what works for one person doesn't always work for another); rather, it's a collection of helpful hints, practical tips and informed advice that you can learn from and adopt to fit your own family's individual circumstances.

I'm thrilled with this book, and I hope that it will serve you well as a valuable reference guide for years to come. My sincere wish is that it will help you simplify your life just a bit, and let you enjoy the time you spend with your family to the fullest extent possible. Enjoy!

Mike Patriarca
Quill President

Introduction

For women who juggle the responsibilities of work, home, and family, there are dozens of decisions we need to make every day, large and small. And it isn't always obvious which of those decisions are truly important and will have long-lasting implications. For example, as hard as it is to deal with the rolling eyes and the *Oh, Mom's,* how we discipline our children will help make them into the people they will be for the rest of their lives.

One of the toughest things about balancing work and family is that moment at the end of the day when you walk in the front door. It's easy to put down the briefcase or cell phone but it's not always so easy to let go of thinking or worrying about work. When you've crossed that welcome mat, you have to find a way to forget about work and focus on your family. You probably need to prepare dinner and your kids need you, although they don't necessarily need you to do anything. They need you just to be—be who you are, be with them, and be present in the moment. After a long day of work, transitioning to that other you may be one of the biggest challenges of your day.

Even the small decisions you make for your family may be at least as important as the decisions you make at work. For example, figuring out what your family eats for dinner tonight might not be of earth-shattering importance, but the kinds of meals your family eats over the course of the many months and years will truly shape what your family will look like. Mom was right about eating your vegetables. Your long-term eating habits could influence how you see yourself, how others see you, and how healthy you are for the rest of your life.

There are books that promise to change your life or fix all your problems in 7 easy steps—this one doesn't. We know that there aren't enough hours in the day to do all we need to do, and nobody has the time or resources to get expert advice as we make each of our daily decisions. The people who give us advice—our parents, siblings, friends, and colleagues—want to help us, but sometimes their advice isn't as good as it could be. Mom wants to remind you that you need more sleep and your best friend considers herself an expert on raising children, but are they well-informed or just opinionated? It would make our lives so much easier if we had someone to advise us—for free and at our convenience any hour of the day or night—who was knowledgeable on all topics, but not someone whose feelings we had to worry about offending if we chose not to listen.

The purpose of this book is to provide that kind of expert advice, based on research rather than opinionated friends or TV experts, so that you can use the information to make your life easier and better. Some of this information will be very useful to you and some may not be relevant to your life at all. Each chapter is about a different topic that is important to many working moms, as well as working dads, grandparents, and even to single men and women who have busy lives with much to juggle.

We hope you will find the book helpful. We expect that some of the information will be new to you, while some you will already know. Some of our suggestions won't necessarily fit with what you want to do or how you like to do things. We offer this book in the spirit of giving you information that you can use to help you manage your work and family responsibilities and help you decide what is best for you and the people you care about.

Here are some highlights:

Organizing My Home and Life

Don't you wish you could wave a magic wand to make everything in your life fall into place? If we delegate tasks and throw away stuff that is no longer needed, it's amazing how much easier our lives can be. This chapter provides tips and suggestions you may find helpful.

Reducing Stress for a Healthier You and a Healthier Family

You have a deadline to meet, the kids need a ride to soccer practice, and you're having guests for the weekend. Stress can push us to perform when needed, but ongoing mental stress can take a big toll on our health and well-being. We'll talk about what you can do to stop that from happening to you.

Rise and Shine: Getting Enough Sleep

We work long hours, we have lots of responsibilities at home, and late at night there is so much temptation to shop online, relax in front of the TV, or get just a little more work done. As a result, adults and children are getting less sleep than the previous generation, and less than they need to work productively, learn easily, and think clearly. If we all can get the sleep we need, we will be more patient, witness less road rage, and our children will do better in school. This chapter will tell you how lack of sleep clouds your judgment even if you think you are fine, and what you can do to get the sleep you need.

Choosing the Right Child Care

Most families need child care at least a few hours a week, and many need child care for 40 hours a week or more. Selecting good child care takes time you don't have, but picking the right care will give your child lifelong advantages. This chapter explains what we know about child care and how it will affect your child, and helps you pick the best childcare arrangement for your children.

How Can I Teach My Kids to Behave?

Have you ever argued with a spouse or parent about the way you discipline your children—or don't discipline them? Is punishment always bad? Can rewarding good behavior make our children too spoiled? Parents often disagree with each other, grandparents and other family members want to tell you why your child needs to be disciplined differently, and even the experts don't always agree. We cut through the controversies to explain what works, what doesn't, and what we teach our children by how we discipline them.

Healthy Eating for Families

The good news is that there is a lot of good food to eat, and much of it is already prepared. All you have to do is buy it and eat it. The bad news is that there is more childhood obesity and diabetes than ever before. We need to find eating habits that satisfy our appetites in ways that will help ensure that our children (and ourselves!) live at least as long as our parents did. This chapter has useful tips on how to stay healthy and prevent your family from becoming overweight, and simple ways to lose some pounds and keep them off.

Kids, TV, and Video Games

TV can be a great teacher—helping your child learn the alphabet and numbers and what is going on in the world. It can also teach words and ideas that you don't like at all. TV is a popular babysitter in homes across America, but just as you wouldn't let a stranger babysit your child, you shouldn't let your children watch programs you haven't checked out first. And, if you are thinking about letting your child have a TV in her bedroom, read this chapter first!

Tips to Keep You and Your Family Healthy

As a working mom, you have a lot on your plate. Just when things are going smoothly, somebody might get sick and suddenly life is so much more complicated. If you're not a doctor or not married to one—and even if you are—the information in this chapter can save you worry, time, and money and make your life much easier.

Back to School: Getting Off on the Right Foot

New Year's Day may be on January 1, but for families with children the year really starts when the school year begins in August or September. Start the year off right by reading this chapter and organizing yourself for the school year ahead. If the school year has already begun, that's okay. Reading this chapter can help make the rest of the year better.

Kids and the Internet

Your kids belong to the Internet generation which means they spend a lot of time in front of that screen. Are they doing their homework, playing a game, instant messaging their friends, or talking to strangers? You can't control everything, but this chapter will help you keep your children safe and help them use the Internet to their best advantage.

Finding Time for Yourself (and Your Special Other) in a Hectic World

You've taken care of everyone else. Now it's time to take care of you. Here are some tips to help you find time to relax and do the things you want to do. And, if you have a significant other, this chapter will help boost that relationship, too.

Caring for an Aging Parent

They call us the sandwich generation, because so many of us are taking care of our children at the same time we are taking care of aging or ailing parents or other relatives. Naming it after a picnic food does not make it a picnic, unfortunately. If you are caring for young and old and are feeling overwhelmed, many chapters in this book contain valuable information for you, but this chapter provides some advice specifically about assisting parents who are increasingly dependent on you.

The Single Parent: Riding a Bicycle Built for Two...Alone

There are unique challenges to being on your own as a mom (or dad). This entire book will be helpful to you, but this chapter provides a little extra advice and special support.

Plan B: What to Do in an Emergency or When Things Don't Go as Planned

You're on a roll, everything is going smoothly, and then suddenly it isn't. If you plan in advance and learn what health problems require immediate medical attention, you won't need to go into a tailspin when a sitter cancels or your child wakes up during the night with a fever. This chapter will guide you in coming up with backup plans so that mild illnesses are less disruptive, and it will help you better decide how to respond to a health emergency.

Help for the Holidays

The holiday season is a wonderful, yet chaotic, time for most families. This chapter includes easy ways to increase the wonder and decrease the stress for your family during the holidays.

Being a working mom is not for the faint of heart! Some day, you will look back and wonder how you did it all. And, you'll even miss how it felt to be the center of your child's world, as challenging as that can be. This book is designed to help you meet those challenges so you can feel great when you look back—you did it all, and you did it amazingly well.

Chapter One

Organizing My Home and Life

Shawna often watches home-makeover shows on TV like "Clean Sweep" and finds herself wishing the producers would pick her house. She can picture it now: They would arrive like a SWAT team and rescue her house from the mess it's become. Cheerful and energetic, they would organize everything in her house for her, and somehow it would stay that way "happily ever after." Deep down, Shawna knows that making the fairy tale come true is up to her—and her family.

If you think you could accomplish so much more if only you were more organized, you are not alone. Millions of people would love to be better organized, but hectic schedules and competing priorities often prevent us from attaining that goal. You have probably heard people say, "If you want to get something done, ask a busy person." Working moms are the busiest folks around, so you can get organized. You just have to start small, keep it simple, and keep reminding yourself that getting organized is going to make your life a whole lot easier. Be patient and realistic: Rome wasn't built in a day, and your house may never look perfect, but you can make improvements that you'll feel good about.

Getting started

The first step to organization is planning and creating a system that works for you. Sure, it sounds like another item on your "To Do" list, but this can be a fun process. When you plan carefully, you can save time and create simple solutions to everyday problems. Everyone has a role in making the home less chaotic, so include your whole family.

▸ Make a list of your family's daily activities and goals. In order to see the big picture, try to be as specific as you can. Include all the things you have to do, such as the carpool for your child's activities, dates and times for doctors' appointments, meal times, bath time, bed time, grocery shopping, meetings, etc.

▸ Don't forget to add the fun things too, like favorite TV shows, manicures, sports, and going out to dinner.

▸ Now, prioritize your activities and place them on a monthly calendar or family bulletin board. This helps you sort your immediate priorities from things that can wait.

▸ Consider making your organizational chart a centralized source for information, by including phone numbers, addresses and e-mails.

  – Then, ask yourself, "Where do I waste the most time?" Is it looking for keys, eyeglasses, phone numbers, or your child's soccer uniform? Remove these stressful time-wasting activities from your life by creating simple solutions that can produce big results. For example, if you misplace your keys, buy a key hook and place your keys there. Teach your children to place belongings in designated areas, which could be baskets, drawers or shelves for each family member, near the entrance to your home or anywhere they are needed.

> If each person in the family has a little "cubby" where his or her things—like cell phones, school papers, purses—can be stored temporarily, then the house will be much less cluttered. You can ask everyone to clean their cubby at the end of the week (just like at school), which means putting items no longer in use back to where they are regularly kept. There may be some grumbling but eventually, everyone will see the benefits of organization and it will become a family routine.

> Aha! Moments: Keep a pad of paper beside your bed, in the kitchen or wherever you feel its best to jot things down. This will help you remember that great idea later. Notepads are less likely to get lost than scrap paper.

> Keep a grocery list on the refrigerator door so that when things run out, you can jot them down easily. This will save time on food shopping.

Everything has its place

It is OK to throw away your son's drawing from 2nd grade. Now that he's in 10th grade, he won't be offended. Put away just a few favorites and toss the rest. If you don't de-clutter, you risk losing the important things, or becoming overrun by piles of stuff!

Here Are a Few Helpful Tips:

➤ Plastic storage bins are great for family mementos, children's old school projects and clothes. Put these bins away and commit to an annual purge.

➤ Keep frequently used items in convenient locations. Put seasonal items in storage.

➤ Have a special place for personal papers such as Social Security cards, tax statements, or your children's immunization records.

➤ Consider a safety deposit box for birth certificates, passports, marriage certificates, and other important documents. You should also keep appliance manuals and warranties handy.

➤ Have a designated place for unpaid bills. Make a monthly schedule for paying your bills and stick to it! Throw away junk mail; don't leave it on the counter for later. The rule is: handle it once and for all and don't mix the bills with junk mail!

➤ Include the kids when packing away old toys and items no longer in use. Consider donating them to charity. This helps de-clutter your home while helping others less fortunate, and teaches your children a great life lesson.

➤ Don't hesitate to throw things away! Not everything needs to be saved. Most of us know in our gut which things should be kept or tossed. Be willing to part with it, especially if it is broken, or hasn't been used in the last year.

➤ Get into the habit of picking up after yourself and putting things back in their rightful places. If you can't pick up and put away as you go, be sure to designate a time each week for this, and have everyone pitch in.

Involve the kids

Getting organized should be a family affair. Teach your children how to put away toys and clean their rooms and play areas. With young children, it helps to have a clean-up song. Make the tune "catchy" (or you can give an old tune new words), and it is okay if the words are silly. The idea is for your children to see clean-up as a natural extension of play. Pretty soon, instead of nagging, you can just start humming the clean-up song and more often than not, they will get the message and get to work.

Have patience, be persistent, and work together as a family to decide who will organize what. You can assign each family member regular tasks and then rotate those tasks periodically. For instance, if you and your family come up with a system for storing and organizing photos—the ones you take and the ones other people give you—you can assign this task to your 11-year-old for six months and then pass it on to your 15-year-old next. Giving your children these responsibilities will make them more mature and give them a sense of pride. When they help manage the household, children learn respect for their home, time and each other. Your children will come to understand that pitching in and staying organized means having more free time for fun and family activities. Start early and these lessons will carry them through life.

Be flexible

Your goals and priorities will change over time, so remain flexible as you organize. Organizing your life and home is like raising kids—plan on dedicating a little extra time and energy upfront and the end result will be worthwhile! Getting organized gets easier with time. Remember, busy families do best when they help one another with the responsibilities of the home. Let's live and work smarter, not harder!

It's been a couple of months since Shawna has tuned into any of the home makeover shows. Instead of watching, she's been doing. For a week, she and her family brainstormed after dinner about how to simplify things, get rid of stuff, and organize their schedules and belongings better. Every Saturday they've been devoting an hour as a family to carrying out the plan, and afterwards they've rewarded themselves by going to the movies, bicycle riding, or another fun activity. Tomorrow, the Goodwill truck comes to pick up the last bag of clothes and toys. Looking around, Shawna hardly recognizes her house. It may not be TV-ready but it's now a place she enjoys coming home to.

Chapter

Two

Reducing Stress For a Healthier You and a Healthier Family

Liz had too much to do. Her parents were moving and needed her help, her daughter was practicing for her major speaking role in the school play, and Liz had just been promoted at work. This was all good news, but it was a lot to juggle. After lots of long days and nonstop weekends, finally, her parents were settled in their new home, her daughter's play was over and she was basking in her success, and Liz was feeling comfortable in her new job. She went to bed feeling relieved but she woke up with the flu.

Can stress make you sick? Yes it can, but there are things you can do to prevent that from happening.

What you need to know about stress

Any challenge—or anything that seems like a challenge or a problem—can cause stress. Even wonderful events, such as a marriage or promotion, can cause stress. The event can be physical, such as breaking an arm. It can be emotional, such as a divorce or the illness or recovery of a family member. Even watching a movie or riding a roller coaster can cause stress, but we usually think of those relatively brief activities as thrilling rather than stressful. The body's reaction to stress happens naturally, and can help us cope with a dangerous or difficult situation. But, if the stress continues, it can harm our health.

When you are faced with stress, your body naturally responds with a "fight or flight" reaction—to either defend yourself or run away from the problem. Hormones such as adrenaline and cortisol increase your energy, heart rate, and blood pressure to pump blood to your muscles. That can be very helpful if you need to run away from a dangerous animal or lift a heavy object that fell on a family member. Who hasn't heard of the mother whose adrenaline gave her the strength to lift a car in order to save her child? These hormones, however, can harm you if you are exposed to them for a long time. Sometimes the stress doesn't go away, such as with the challenges of demanding children or a very ill family member.

In the long run, the hormones from stress will weaken your immune system, so you can't fight off viruses and bacteria as easily. You might be more likely to develop gastrointestinal conditions such as ulcers and irritable bowel syndrome. You might also develop high blood pressure, stroke, or heart disease. Even wounds will heal more slowly. For example, a study found that women caring for mentally disabled family members took an average of 9 days longer to heal a small surgical wound, compared to other women with the same kind of wound.[1] Even arguments with your spouse can make a wound take up to a day longer to heal.[2]

Men and women who spend a lot of time taking care of sick relatives or friends have high cortisol levels and so their immune system is weakened. When men and women who took care of Alzheimer's disease patients were given flu shots, the shots were not as effective in preventing flu as they were for men and women who were not taking care of Alzheimer's patients.

The information in this chapter is important for anyone who takes care of others, whether children or adults. If you don't ask for help when you need it, you risk getting sick and not being able to provide your family with the support they count on. Whenever you catch yourself saying, "I'll grab something to eat after I go to the school meeting and get the kids into bed," or "If I stay up a little later, I can get all these bills taken care of," stop, take a deep breath and think about the oxygen masks on airplanes. Remember the announcement about them? It tells parents to first place the masks over their own faces before attending to their children. That's because if parents don't protect themselves first, they can't take care of others.

Coping with stress

Men and women tend to cope with stress differently. Research shows that the support of friends can help women cope with stress better than it helps men.[3] The support from friends helps enhance the immune system and makes women more resistant to disease. For example, a diagnosis of breast cancer is very stressful, and women with breast cancer who have strong social supports from friends or relatives tend to live longer than women who don't have strong supports. We don't know why, but research also shows that the support provided by women is more effective at lowering blood pressure in both men and women than the support provided by men.[4]

Unfortunately, many women have trouble coping with stress. Women are three times as likely to become depressed as a reaction to stress, compared to men.

What Can You Do to Beat Stress?
This is What Works:

Exercise! Physical exertion releases endorphins, which can make you feel better and boost your immune system. It also helps reduce depression.

You may need to change your thinking about exercise. Often we give up on it because we are too ambitious or have too many expectations for what it can do for us. Even moderate, perspiration-free exercise offers health benefits. No pain and still you gain by reducing your stress levels.

You are what you eat! A balanced diet can help your body respond to stress. Reducing caffeine can also help. People who consume more caffeine (from coffee, tea, some types of sodas, chocolate, or other foods) have higher levels of stress hormones and experience more stress. Eat at regular intervals rather than waiting for severe hunger pangs. Try to treat your body with the same loving tenderness you would give your newborn baby. You were so good at anticipating her every need and it's important to remember to respond with the same good instincts to your own.

Get your Zzzzs! Most adults need 8–9 hours of sleep each night, but few of us manage to get that much. When we don't get the sleep we need, we become more vulnerable to stress, which then makes it more difficult to sleep, much the way an overtired infant has trouble falling asleep or an overly excited toddler gets more revved up the longer he goes without his nap. Don't let yourself get trapped in a cycle of too much awake time. Make your own "bedtime" a priority just as you would with your children. Find a schedule and a soothing routine and stick to it.

Express yourself! Researchers have found that expressing emotions to friends or family, or even writing down feelings, can help reduce stress. Write a letter to your overbearing boss or the relative who made a hurtful remark at the family picnic. You don't have to mail it. (In fact, mailing it could be very stressful.) Just getting the emotions "out" can be a huge relief.

▶

Ask for help! Remember that you can't always do it all. If you're feeling overwhelmed, seek help from friends, family, or a professional.

Less worry—more action! Worrying is a part of being a parent, but try to cut down on worrying about things you can't control and things that aren't that important. If you have a problem, try to work out a solution in small steps. Focus on what you can do, not on what might go wrong.

Stuck in bed with the flu, Liz decided to make some changes. There were always going to be surprises, deadline crunches, and times during the year when everything seems to happen at once. Liz accepted these as facts of life but decided that from now on she would take a little time for herself every day to just relax. She also realized she has to be better about saying "no" when she really can't take on another task, and that it is better to ask her friends or family for help when she needs it, rather than automatically going into crisis mode. Three months later, Liz is amazed at how these small changes have helped her at work and at home.

Chapter

Three

Rise and Shine: Getting Enough Sleep

When Christina's alarm clock went off this morning, she immediately hit the snooze button like she always does. Ten minutes later, Christina drags herself out of bed and heads to the kitchen to make a big pot of coffee. On the way, she stops at her son's bedroom and lets him know it is time to wake up and get ready for school.

*After finishing her first cup of coffee, Christina is about to take a shower when she realizes her son is still fast asleep. She thinks, "We're going to be late **again**."*

A couple of hours later, Christina is sitting in a staff meeting at work. She feels her eyes closing. It feels so good, like wrapping yourself in a warm blanket on a winter day. But suddenly, there's applause and, with a jerk of her head, she awakes. She looks around. It seems like Bob's presentation went well—but did anyone notice her sleeping through it?

Are you and your family getting enough sleep?

When it is time to get up in the morning, do you hit the snooze button to get another 5 or 10 minutes of sleep? Do other family members need repeated prodding to get out of bed? Do the adults in your family rely on coffee, cola, or other forms of caffeine throughout the day to stay alert? These rituals are not much fun for you or for others in your family who are coping with bleary eyes and fatigue.

Why does every minute of sleep seem so precious in the morning but not at night? How does our morning routine tell us if everyone in our family is getting enough sleep to be productive, healthy, and avoid accidents?

Studies show that sleep deprivation is rampant, and we are getting less sleep than previous generations.[1] Kids are getting much less sleep than is recommended.[2] Most of us are getting up at about the same time in the morning as adults and children always have—it's that everyone is going to sleep later. Some blame too many scheduled activities, too much stimulation and too much caffeine. Others blame our "24-hour-a-day, seven-day-a-week" lifestyle, which makes it possible to do almost anything at any hour, including watching TV, shopping, catching up on work, and emailing friends.

There was a time, of course, when our activities were limited by light. Now we have light whenever we want it and can take our work and distractions with us wherever we go, thanks to cell phones, computers, and other electronic devices. The price for all this wonderful flexibility seems to be sleep, and we are, as it turns out, paying dearly. Getting too little sleep leads to injuries and behavioral problems in school-age children[3, 4], poorer grades[5], and contributes to obesity[6].

How does lack of sleep affect us?

Learning. Students are less able to pay attention or remember what they are learning in school when they do not get enough sleep. A sleep-deprived adult is less impressive at work or in social situations, sometimes slurring words, speaking in a monotone voice, or speaking at a slower (boring!) pace. Studies show that sleep-deprived people are less able to make good decisions quickly, and less able to multi-task.[7]

Safety. Studies of students and adults show that people who are sleep-deprived have a more difficult time reacting well while driving or at work.[8] Lack of sleep has a similar effect as alcohol on judgment and reaction time.[9] And as with alcohol, the teen or adult who is impaired from lack of sleep may not realize it. In fact, many people who do not get enough sleep experience "sleep attacks"—unintentionally falling asleep for a few seconds. Sleep attacks might mean you miss some information if you're sitting in class or watching TV, but can be fatal if you are driving.

Dr. David Dinges, a professor at the University of Pennsylvania, conducted a study that allowed adults to sleep only 6 hours each night.[10] After a week, the adults in the study were just as impaired as adults getting 8 hours of sleep per night who are then forced to go without sleep for 48 hours straight! This may surprise you, since staying up all night feels much worse than getting six hours of sleep each night. It's an important lesson for all of us, and especially teenagers who need even more sleep than adults and would probably be even more impaired by 6 hours of sleep.

Smoking, drinking, and drugs. The impaired judgment that can cause car accidents also can result in making bad choices. As we all know, teens can be easily swayed by peer pressure, and lack of sleep makes them even less able to "just say no" or think ahead about negative consequences.

Conflicts with family and friends. Tired babies are cranky, and research shows that tired teens and adults are cranky, too. This can contribute to constant tension and arguments between teens and other family members, as well as road rage, gang fights, family violence, and other serious problems.

Health. Over time, sleep deprivation can weaken the immune system. White blood cells, which are needed to fight infections and illness of any kind, will decrease in number and in activity. Sleep is important for regulating your hormones and metabolism, which is basically your body's engine. Lack of sleep slows our bodies down, making them burn fewer calories, while increasing our appetites. Less than four hours of sleep a night produces changes in the body that are similar to the effects of aging[11], which may be why too little sleep seems to increase the chances of weight gain, hypertension, and Type 2 diabetes. These health problems can start early: infants who average less than 12 hours sleep a day are twice as likely to be overweight by age 3, compared to children who sleep longer.[12]

Why it matters. It's never too early (or too late) to develop good sleep habits. Make sleep a priority for your children and for you, because you are the one who sets the example. If your kids know you don't get enough sleep, they will think that sleep just isn't that important. Sleep isn't just important—it's a life-saver. Some of the biggest accidents in our lifetime—from the grounding of the Exxon Valdez oil tanker, to the nuclear reactor accidents at Chernobyl and Three Mile Island, to the explosion of the Challenger space shuttle[13]—are believed to have occurred because the people in charge weren't getting enough shut-eye. So take charge and re-charge with some of those well-deserved ZZZs.

How much sleep is enough?

According to experts, the amount of necessary sleep varies from person to person—but it doesn't vary as much as people think it does. Our friends and relatives may believe they can breeze through their days on just a few hours of slumber, but research shows that they may not be functioning as well as they think. They may even fall asleep for a second while driving—not enough to notice, but enough to cause an accident if it happens at just the wrong time. Experts tell us that most people need between 8 and 9 hours, and would get that much sleep if they didn't know what time it was and were allowed to sleep as long as they want.

Instead, many adults get 7 hours or less of sleep each night, think-ing that is enough for them. But, research shows that our work performance, driving, ability to cope with stress, patience with our kids and co-workers—just about every aspect of our daily life—is harmed because 7 hours is simply not enough sleep to do our best. Just one more hour of sleep per night would mean we are less likely to lose our temper, less likely to have a car accident, and less likely to make a mistake at work. In addition to everything else, sleep helps our memory.[14]

If you're not sure if you need more sleep, here's a clue: people who have enough sleep at night do not fall asleep during the day, even during a boring lecture or TV program.

What about your kids?

The average kid today has a very busy day. There's school, play dates, playing sports or games, and doing homework. Our kids need enough sleep to give their bodies and minds a rest.

Most kids between first and fifth grades get about 9.5 hours of sleep a night, but experts agree they need 10 or 11 hours each night. "While the amount of sleep necessary drops once kids reach adolescence," says Judith Owens, associate professor of pediatrics at Brown University and a noted expert on childhood sleep disorders, "They still need at least nine hours under ideal circumstances." How do we know how much sleep they need? In their studies, sleep researchers let kids fall asleep and wake up naturally, without any information about what time it was. They found that teenagers slept an average of just over 9 hours. Studies also show that kids' "biological clocks" change as they reach adolescence, causing them to want to go to bed later and sleep later when they are teenagers.[15]

Sleeping late on weekends can help children and adults make up for lack of sleep the night before, but it can't compensate for ongoing, long-term sleep deprivation. That's because, according to the National Academy of Sciences, if we constantly get too little sleep, we lose our ability to make up for it.[16] "Sleeping in" on the weekend can also make it more difficult to go to sleep on Sunday night. It's like changing time zones every week. Sleep experts recommend not letting your weekend sleep schedule vary from your weekday schedule by more than two hours. For example, if you need to get up at 7:00 am during the week, get up by 9:00 am on weekends.

Parents need to set consistent rules about bedtime. If we enforce these rules with young children, it will be easier to maintain them as our children grow up. And, if we enforce the rules every day it is easier to not give in some days. Giving in just makes your children more likely to test those limits every day.

Tips to Get Your Child to Sleep

For most kids, sleeping comes pretty naturally. Here are some tips to help your children catch all the ZZZs they need:

➤ Try to get them to go to bed at the same time every night. This helps their body get into a routine.

➤ Follow a bedtime routine that is calming, such as giving your child a warm bath or reading a relaxing book.

➤ Limit foods and drinks that contain caffeine, especially toward the end of the day. In addition to coffee, these include colas, some other soft drinks, chocolate, and tea, for example. That means no chocolate cake before bed!

➤ Keep their rooms TV-free. Research shows that kids who have a TV in their room sleep less. If there is a TV that you can't remove, turn it off when it is time to sleep.

➤ Make sure children don't watch scary TV shows or movies shortly before bedtime. The excitement or fear from these programs can make it difficult for kids to fall asleep. If the show is really "must-see" TV for your kids, tape or TiVo the show and let them watch it during the day.

➤ Use the bed just for sleeping—not for doing homework, reading, playing games, or talking on the phone. That way, children will train their bodies to associate their bed with sleep.

So, how do we make sure Mom and Dad get enough sleep?

Most of the rules that apply to kids, apply to parents, too. If you want to get more sleep, you may have to plan for it. Start by limiting the number of caffeinated beverages you drink in a day. Many of us come to rely on these and other stimulants, such as the nicotine in cigarettes, to stay awake or for a quick "pick-me-up." Remember that coffee and colas aren't the only drinks with lots of caffeine—Mountain Dew and Red Bull have even more, and chocolate has caffeine too. As a result, many of us feel wide-awake at night, just when we should be winding down. Most of us go to sleep too late and then need caffeine to feel alert the next morning—starting the cycle all over again.

What you could do to fall asleep easily:

Have a bedtime ritual. This sends a cue to your body that it is time to settle down and fall asleep. A ritual does not have to be a long process and can be as simple as brushing your teeth and reading for 15 minutes.

Keep a regular sleeping pattern. This allows your body's biological clock to take care of your ability to fall asleep and insures that you will be alert during the appropriate times of the day. One way to help set your biological clock is to spend 15 minutes in direct sunlight soon after you wake up in the morning, prompting your body to tune in to the time of day. If you can't have breakfast in the sun, walk your child to school, or walk to work, try to find a way to get some sunlight in the morning. (And, the Vitamin D from a few minutes of sunlight is good for your health for other reasons, too.)

Avoid going to bed hungry. This will let you sleep soundly though the night without waking up from hunger pangs. Eating a heavy meal close to bedtime will make it difficult to fall asleep, so time your meals carefully, but a light snack is usually fine.

Unwind earlier in the evening, taking the time to relax your body and mind. Falling asleep can be almost impossible if your mind is racing or working through problems, weighing decisions and reviewing the day past or upcoming. A calm, clear mind is necessary for a relaxed body.

Take a warm bath before going to bed. Warm baths raise your body's temperature. After the bath your body cools off, and this cooling is what makes you sleepy.

Christina arrives home at the end of her work day feeling like she hadn't done her best. She had been cranky at work and felt overwhelmed. She wondered whether her boss had seen her nod off during the staff meeting. Kicking off her shoes, she says to herself, "What a wake-up call! I need to get more sleep."

This time, she really means it. As she's getting dinner ready, she starts to pour a glass of Diet Coke but catches herself and switches to a drink without caffeine. After the family finishes eating, she makes sure to get her son into bed on time. She reads him a favorite story, kisses him good-night, and shuts off the light. Instead of watching reruns on TV or checking her email, she pays a few bills, gets everything ready for the next day, and gets into bed. Her head sinks into the pillow and she smiles, realizing that she feels surprisingly relaxed and sleepy.

Chapter Four

Choosing the Right Child Care

Beth and her family recently moved to a new area. The family is excited about their new home and is looking forward to meeting new friends. But Beth is wondering what child care arrangement will be best for her youngest son. As a working mom, Beth needs help with child care, but she is not sure what kind of place would be best for her child or even how to begin her search.

How many moms and dads think that looking for child care is one of a parent's toughest jobs? The answer is that many parents feel this way. In fact, during the past two decades, there has been a big increase in the number of families with two parents working outside the home. Three out of every five children under six-years-old are regularly cared for by people other than their parents—at a child care center, preschool, in their own homes, relatives' homes, or in family run day care homes.[1] The quality of child care varies tremendously. How can you make the best choice for your child and your family?

In choosing child care, parents are choosing the world where their children will spend much of their time—a world that influences who that child will become. Child care can provide interesting, educational, and fun experiences that are different from the experiences a child has with parents. Choosing the right child care takes time, but in the long run it will make your life much easier. This chapter will help you in your search for the child care that works best for your family.

What Are the Different Types of Child Care?

> **In-home care:** the caregiver comes to your home and cares for your child there.

> **Family child care:** you take your child to the home of the caregiver.

> **Center-based care:** you take your child to a place that is organized and staffed specifically to care for a group or groups of children.

What's best for infants and toddlers?

Children thrive in loving and stimulating environments. In the ideal world, young children would spend many waking hours each day with loving family members, but in the real world, parents have to juggle financial needs, job demands, and family responsibilities. Every family must determine what is best for all its members. A predictable routine from loving and responsive caregivers is what very young children need most—even if some of the people providing the care are not related to the child.

Some parents arrange for child care in their own home by a baby-sitter. Others arrange care in the home of a relative, neighbor, or friend. Even when parents know the child care provider, they need to make sure that he or she is experienced in providing child care and likes spending many hours a day with children. If you are considering leaving your child in the care of someone you know personally but don't have direct experience with as a child care provider, you should ask for references and speak to a few of the families that have hired this person to take care of their children.

Other options include a child care center or a family day care home. Day care centers and family day care homes are licensed or regulated by state agencies. However, having a license only means that the center or home has complied with very basic standards of health and safety. Licensing or registration doesn't mean that the activities offered are appropriate or engaging, or that the providers are meeting children's developmental needs. It also doesn't mean that the child care workers are well-trained or experienced.[2] Parents have to figure out for themselves if the care offered in these centers will nurture their child and provide a truly safe, healthy, and stimulating environment. Knowing what to look for can help you make sure that your child's day care experience is positive and will help him get ready for kindergarten.

Health and safety are first and foremost

Health and safety are the "must have" ingredients of any child care arrangement, whether it is baby-sitting, family day care, or a center-based program. Next, you want to make sure that the child care you are considering provides the building blocks for learning. The person caring for your child should be able to spend some one-on-one time with each child, and the setting should look inviting, with sufficient toys, books and other resources. Children who get little attention in day care will be demanding and unhappy at home, and may have behavior problems later as well. The better the child care, the better your child will learn vocabulary words and develop other basic skills, including the ability to get along with other children.

Choosing the "right" child care is very important, but there is reassuring news. The latest studies show that the stimulation, attention, and caring that children get at home are still the most important influences on their learning and behavior.[3]

When choosing child care—whether it's at a relative's house, a family day care home, or a child care center—the most important thing is the quality of the care. Of course the big question is: What is "high quality care," and how can you measure something as subjective as quality? Obviously, some adults are more loving and nurturing and fun with children than others. Even so, it is possible to measure quality in three ways.

Quality care: what to look for

Ratio of caregivers to children. One adult can't take good care of more than three infants, or four or five very young children, even if the children are napping a lot of the day.[4] (See chart on page 26 for the adult-to-child ratio for children of different ages.)

Caregiver and child interaction. How much time do the child care staff spend talking to and playing with the children? Educational TV programs, DVDs or videotapes are not appropriate for children under two and are *never* a good substitute for adults playing with and talking to children one-on-one.

Children's movement and play. Children should be free to move and play safely. This means that babies should spend very little waking time in cribs, car seats, or "jumpy seats" by themselves. On the other hand, toddlers and older children should not be wandering around aimlessly. Young children learn by playing—with toys, other children or adults—and by imitating the children and adults they spend time with.

Things to Consider When Choosing Child Care

According to the American Academy of Pediatrics, there are several factors that you want to consider when making your child care decision:

Location. How far is the child care from home? From your work? Is this convenient for both parents? Can either parent get there quickly in an emergency?

Hours. What hours of care are available? What happens if you are late in picking up your child? Is care available on holidays? Is there a time of the year when the center shuts down for vacation or when parents need to make other child care arrangements?

Licensing and accreditation. Is the center or family run day care home licensed by the necessary local government agencies? Or is it registered? Have there been violations, and if so, what and when were they? Is the program currently accredited or seeking to get accredited? If so, by which organization?

Inspections and consultations. Is there a doctor, nurse or other qualified health professional who serves as a consultant for the child care program? (The national standard is that center-based infant-toddler programs should be visited by a health professional at least once a month, and all other child care programs should be visited at least quarterly.)

Visiting policy. Are you welcome to visit during normal operating hours before and after enrolling your child? Are you able to visit all the areas your child will use?

Caregiver experience and training. What education, training and experience do the caregiver or center director and staff have? Has the staff had training recently (during the past year)? Who is providing the training—is it given by other staff or by outside experts?

Adequate staffing — Are there enough trained adults taking care of the children every day, even when a staff member is ill or on vacation? What about during naps? Here are the nationally recognized standards:

▶

Age	Child-Staff Ratio	Maximum Group Size
Birth–12 months	3:1	6
13–30 months	4:1	8
31–35 months	5:1	10
3-year-olds	7:1	14
4–5-year-olds	8:1	16
6–8-year-olds	10:1	20
9–12-year-olds	12:1	24

How to help your children adjust

Almost 12 million of the more than 18 million children younger than five years of age in the U.S. are in some form of regular child care.[5] This means that millions of parents are finding ways to help their children adjust to being away from mom or dad and get used to a new routine and situation.

The age of your child will affect how she adapts to child care. In the first seven months of life, most infants warm up to caring adults quickly and seldom have problems adjusting to good child care. Infants older than this may be upset when left with strangers. They may feel separation anxiety, which is a normal part of development for some children. They will need a little extra time and some help from you to get to know the caregiver. To help prepare your young child for care, parents can play "peek-a-boo" or other games where they disappear and then, to the child's great delight, reappear. These games show your child that even though family members and friends go away, they return. Before going to the store or out on errands, assure even the smallest child, "Mommy (or Daddy) goes out, but she always comes back."

When you leave your child in someone else's care, remember that the way you say goodbye is very important. When it's time to leave, don't look hesitant or worried, and fight the temptation to linger. Saying a quick, upbeat good-bye will help your child adjust more quickly. Have a special routine to help your child feel secure and make the transition easier. This might be exchanging a hug and kiss and saying, "See you later alligator."

Spend at least an hour or two watching the daily routine at the day-care setting before you select it. Know how many children are there (and the maximum they will allow) and get to know all the adults who might have contact with your child. If one woman is in charge, find out who provides back-up if he is sick or needs to be away, even for "just a few minutes." Those other caregivers, whether they include a husband, teenage children, or assistants, may be inexperienced or not motivated to care for young children.

To keep things going smoothly in care, stay involved with the child care provider; meet regularly and ask questions to make sure things are going well. The more confident you are, the more relaxed your child is likely to be.

Toddlers may cry, pout, and refuse to go to child care or act angry in other ways. A preschooler, for instance, may start to behave like a younger child—talking in a baby voice or needing a special stuffed animal she hasn't slept or played with in months. Children may even have some toileting accidents or have trouble sleeping. These behaviors usually go away after a few days or weeks in high-quality child care.

There are several things you can do to help your child adjust to a new child care arrangement. Set up a visit with an in-home caregiver while you are at home or when you need child care for a short time. Visit the center or family child care home that you have chosen with your child before beginning care. Show your child that you like and trust the caregiver.

Some children like to carry a reminder of home when they go to child care. A family photograph or small toy can be helpful. Talking to your child about child care and the caregiver can calm his fears. Being prepared makes any new experience easier for children. There also are storybooks about child care that you and your child can read together.

Tips to Make Your Child's Transition Easier:

Give yourself enough time. To avoid rushing, stress, and short tempers in the morning, prepare your child's supplies the night before. You want the day to start as peacefully as possible, so that saying good-bye is easier for both of you.

Plan a gradual transition for the first several mornings. Stay a while during the first few days, or have another person whom your child trusts stay if you cannot. When it is time for you to go, hug your child good-bye, and then leave. If your child cries the first few times, don't worry. That is normal. If you stay during the tears, you just make it more difficult for your child to let you leave. The tears will probably last just a few minutes, and not longer than 20 minutes. You can call later to find out how your child is doing.

Gradually increase the hours spent in child care as part of the transition. If possible, pick your child up before lunch on the first day, after lunch on the second day, then after nap, and finally have your child stay the whole day. If you can't take time from work, perhaps a relative or friend your child knows well can help by picking your child up early for the first few days.

Let your child know if you will be late. Call to let your child know if you will be one of the last parents to arrive at the end of the day. If you will always be one of the last parents to pick up your child, talk about that so your child will know to expect it. If your child is old enough, help her learn to look at the clock and know when to expect you. Suggest that the child care provider spend special time with the last few children, by reading a book, playing a game, drawing or some other activity that is fun for just a few children.

Be patient at pick-up. Picking up your child from day care can sometimes be as challenging as dropping him off. After all, it's another transition so try not to be in a rush. Your child may even act angry or unhappy to see you. Don't take it personally—it may just be that your child needs time to get ready to leave or wants to show you something. Allow a little time for your child to prepare to leave or share something from his day away from you. A minute or two of your undivided attention is usually enough. Also, by meeting your child's friends, talking to the teachers or child care providers, and

▸

spending a little extra time playing with him at the child care center, you are showing your child that you think this is an enjoyable place to be.

Checklist of What is Needed For the First Day:

❏ Health forms and immunization records need to be with the provider

❏ Phone number where you can be reached

❏ A blanket, stuffed animal or other item your child is attached to and will find comfort in

❏ At least one change of clothes, plus rain boots, a hat, sweater, or other items needed if the weather changes or the children will spend time outdoors

❏ Diapers, wipes, or pull-ups if these are needed and not provided by the day care center

❏ Family picture for your child's cubby

❏ And be sure YOU have the phone number for the child care center!

After-school care for elementary school children

After-school programs have to meet the needs of children, parents, schools and communities. Ideally, a good quality after-school program can make a parent's life much easier and provide a child help with school work while fostering self-esteem and friendships and providing a happy and safe environment. Parents should look into the various options: does the school offer on-site after-school care? Do any of the local day care centers offer transportation to pick up children from school? Or perhaps there are neighbors with children of similar ages who might be willing to help out or trade favors. If family members live far away or are unavailable, is there an in-home caregiver recommended by neighbors or friends who can provide after-school care?

Like all child care programs, after-school programs will provide safety and security if they employ enthusiastic and qualified staff who keep children busy and happy. Children need adult supervision after school and should not go home to an empty house. Unfortunately, just as children are getting old enough to seem ready to be home alone—in middle school and during the early teenage years—that is when they can get into trouble with alcohol, drugs, and other risky behaviors if no adults are around to make sure they avoid temptation and resist peer pressure. So, try to keep arrangements in place to continue to provide supervision for young teens, or make plans to keep them busy with organized activities and regularly monitored by you or other family members, neighbors, or other adults that you trust.

Trusting your child care provider and feeling comfortable with the arrangement you've chosen will make your life much easier. You and your child care provider are a team. As a team, you will be a lot stronger if everyone is informed of any new issues at home or changes your child is going through.

Beth asked other moms and dads at her job and in her neighborhood about their child care settings. She also went on the Internet to do research and contacted her local child care resource agency. After visiting a few places, Beth chose a small child care center near her job, so that she can occasionally drop by during her lunch to see her son and observe what the center is like.

Chapter

Five

How Can I Teach My Kids to Behave?

Like many fathers of teenagers, Steve feels embarrassed and even angry when his daughter says, loudly enough for the neighbors to hear, "No, I'm not going to do it!" or "Not now, I'm busy!" It seems like only yesterday she was an adorable toddler struggling with a too-big rake while working alongside him. Steve's wife, Mary, is also frustrated with her daughter's behavior lately. But she is less nostalgic for the "good old days" when she sees her neighbor, Sarah, in the grocery store, trying to convince her four-year-old that running up and down the aisles is not a good idea.

Of course, it's worse when it's your child who is making the fuss. Take a deep breath and remember that all parents have to deal with children's challenging behavior at some point during their child's growth and development.

Tantrums, disobedience, and other bad behaviors are hard to cope with and can be frustrating. At different times in your child's life, toddler or teen, this may be a natural part of your child becoming more independent and testing his or her limits. But, that doesn't mean you have to accept it. You just have to have a plan of action—a plan that will get you through these stressful events and reduce the chances of them happening again.

Remember that it is the behavior that is bad, not the child. Show your child you love her, even though you don't love her behavior.

Equally important to remember is that a parent is not supposed to be a friend. If you are a parent, you need to set the limits and stick with them. See the behaviors you don't like as an opportunity for you to teach your child the difference between right and wrong, and the consequences of both.

Disciplining children of all ages

Discipline is used to help children develop self-control. It means setting limits and correcting misbehavior. Discipline is also used to encourage children, guide them, help them feel good about themselves, and teach them how to think for themselves. Discipline is not the same as punishment. Discipline is all about shaping behaviors while teaching your child right from wrong, how to respect the rights of others, and which behaviors are acceptable and which are not. The goal is a child who feels secure and loved, who is self-confident and self-disciplined, who knows how to control his impulses, and who does not get overly frustrated with the challenges of everyday life.

Modeling good behavior

Parents often get frustrated when children talk back, will not do chores, or whine and scream. Do not let your frustration get out of control. Do not get into a yelling match with your child. If you yell or hit your children, you are teaching them to yell and hit others to get their way. Show your children that you can calmly talk with them about what is bothering you, just as you want them to calmly "use their words" to tell you why they are upset, rather than acting out. Model the good manners and respectful listening that you want your child to develop.

One size does not fit all

Strategies for discipline need to vary according to a child's age, and some children respond better to some techniques than others. However, the basic rules are the same: you want to encourage some behaviors and discourage others. Children crave routine and predictability—from their world and from you, which means you have to be consistent with your rules. Focus on the positive: expect her to be wonderful, and more often than not, she will be. Here are some helpful tips to remember for your children during the different stages of their growth.

Ages 0–2. Children this age want to explore everything—even things that are not safe to touch and places that you want to keep off-limits. When your young child reaches for a lamp cord or looks as if he is going to hit or bite someone, it's best to prevent the hurt rather than scold him afterwards. Place your hand between him and whatever he is aiming for, look him in the eye, and say "no" in a calm but firm manner. If your toddler continues pulling down videos from the shelf after you have told him not to, take him to a different area or get him involved in another form of play.

Be clear about what is acceptable and what isn't. Let your child know it's not okay to tug hair or throw food. If saying no doesn't work and if it seems he is acting up to get a reaction from you, consider a timeout. For a child this young, a minute or two of quiet time in a designated place can help him settle down…and keep you from losing your cool. Anything longer is too long for toddlers.

Ages 3–5. Children between 3 and 5 years old are better able to anticipate and predict things. They are starting to understand that actions have reactions. When your four-year-old misbehaves at the park, you can react by cutting short her playtime. This is a good time to get your child used to the idea that Mom and Dad make the rules and she is expected to follow them or accept the consequences. Being in charge means you have to model the behavior you want from your child. If you want her to touch gently, stroke her softly as you remind her. When your child offers her shovel to a younger one at the sandbox, let her know you noticed by praising her generosity.

One of the best ways to discipline your child is by giving her a task that will help undo or make up for whatever she did wrong—like giving her a sponge and telling her to clean up the finger painting she did…on the wall. If you are having trouble thinking of an appropriate consequence or punishment, or your child seems too wound up to listen to you, consider a timeout. It is appropriate for this age. Find a spot without distractions or toys where she can take some time to think about what just happened, and afterwards spend a minute talking about what she might do differently next time.

Ages 6–8. Being consistent and following through become even more important with children 6–8 years old. They really notice things, are concerned with fairness, and know how to express themselves verbally. They will learn to point out inconsistencies and may whine or argue to get their way. If you want them to follow through with what you ask, you have to follow through and do what you said you would do.

So, avoid making promises you are not likely to deliver on or threats you are not planning to carry out. Similarly, be realistic when stating the punishments for unacceptable behavior. For example, saying, "Put all your toys away this instant or I am never giving you another toy again," is not realistic. Instead you might say, "I am thinking that you have too many toys and that is making clean-up difficult for you. Tomorrow let's store the toys you don't play with that much in a closet. Even toys like to take turns."

Avoid consequences that are out of proportion to the misbehavior, or have no relation to the rule that has been broken. Discipline is not about relieving you of your anger; it's about teaching, and a child can only learn so much from "no dessert for you!"

What to Do? Try a Timeout.

If you want to see how giving children a timeout can work, watch an episode of Supernanny—on TV, on DVD or on the Internet. This Mary Poppins of the digital age uses the "naughty stool" to show children that bad behavior is unacceptable and punished with time on the naughty stool, or some other place such as the stairs or the corner. Timeouts can be useful up until the age of 11 or 12.

Timeout Tips:
A timeout is used immediately after a bad behavior to show children the consequences. It is also a time for them to think about what they have done. After the timeout (experts recommend a minute for every year of your child's age), parents once again:

> explain the reasons for the discipline

> state the behavior that is unacceptable

> ask for an apology from the child

> end the timeout with a hug for the child

Be Consistent!
It's important to be consistent, to use a timeout immediately (no matter how busy you are), and to not back down.

A timeout should never be in a bedroom or other room with fun things to do. That isn't punishment.

Is there an effective "timeout" for teenagers? Most likely it would be time spent without a cell phone, computer, or TV. Or, being "grounded" when they would otherwise spend time with their friends.

Ages 9–12. The older the child is, the more independence and responsibility he can and should handle. Sometimes, the best discipline isn't the kind you dole out but what comes from letting a child experience the consequences of his actions. Parents need to let children make mistakes from time to time. If your child announces just before bedtime that he forgot to do his homework or study for a quiz, you might be tempted to let him stay up late or help him. A good night of sleep along with a low test score or the disappointment in his teacher's face may help him remember better next time.

Ages 13 and up. Most teenagers know the rules but quite a few feel like rules were made to be bent or broken. Even though teens may resist rules, and you may be willing to grant them greater freedom in addition to greater responsibility, they still very much need you to set limits. You have to pick your battles, of course, but when it comes to homework, chores, media use, dating, drugs and curfews, for instance, you need to lay down clear rules. Let your kids know how you feel about these issues. They may sometimes look at you like you are from another planet—if they look at you at all—but don't be fooled: they care what you think.

When you decide to take away privileges after your teen breaks a rule, be sure to discuss why what she did was unacceptable. Let him know you are confident she will use better judgment next time. Kids have to be entrusted to prove they are trustworthy. Likewise, teenagers need to have control over some aspects of their lives—that is important to their growth and development. For example, a parent can allow younger teens to make decisions about some of their clothes, their hairstyle, or how to decorate their room.

Accent the positive; eliminate the negative

The key to discipline is to reward the behaviors you like and discourage the behaviors you don't like. Many parents think of punishment as something that hurts a child. Physical punishment like spanking is opposed by the American Academy of Pediatrics because it is no more effective than gentler types of discipline and gives kids the message that hitting solves problems.[1]

Taking away privileges

The most effective punishment is often taking away something the child wants. It is important to figure out what your child considers a "treasure"—something he will miss if you take it away as a method of discipline. If your child has a lot of toys, he may barely miss one that is taken away. And, if you take away something for too long, children may find other interests—making this discipline ineffective. The key is to take away something important, be consistent, and do not give in early and return the privilege too soon.

For teenagers, the choices are especially limited—the car, video games, TV time, going out with friends. Even so, you need to be just as consistent for teenagers as for young children.

Rewarding good behavior

Most important, be sure to use praise, hugs, and other rewards for the behavior that you like. You can use daily and weekly charts with gold stars to reinforce the kinds of behaviors you want from your young children every day, such as going to bed on time or putting away toys. Use the star system to show your child how her daily accomplishments add up to a more substantial reward, and together you and your child can help decide what that will be.

While you probably won't be using stickers or stars with older teenagers, don't forget to praise and hug them. It may seem like teenagers don't need our positive feedback, but even the most sullen of adolescents appreciates praise from their parents.

Avoid using food and gifts to reward good behavior on a daily basis, —these can cause children to be overweight and demanding. Of course, the occasional use of a more substantial reward (a reasonably priced toy or special treat) is effective for a very important accomplishment—but not for behaviors you expect every day or every week.

Spending quality time with your children

In addition to rewarding specific good behavior, don't forget to make room for quality time with your child. Time spent talking to your child about his day, showing how much you love him, and learning about what's important to him is the fun part of being a parent and also makes discipline easier and more effective for you and your child.

As parents, we have a lot of things competing for our time and attention. Children may want us when we're busy, and when we are ready to spend time with them they may have other things they want to do. Let your children know that you are interested in what is happening in their lives. Notice the times when your children are most likely to talk, for example, at bedtime, before dinner, or in the car. If those times don't work, try to set up a time for weekly one-on-one activities with each child.

When kids want to talk, express interest in what they are saying and listen to their point of view, even if it's difficult to hear. Instead of lecturing, talk to them about their options and help them make the right choice.

Being a parent is a tough job. You need to listen, but also you need to tell them in words and actions what you expect from them.

Steve and Mary understand that raising children is a tough job but also very rewarding. They are working on teaching their kids that if they want certain privileges and greater independence, they have to be responsive and responsible. They are teaching their kids that in addition to their rights, they also have responsibilities. Mary and Sarah get together over coffee and swap discipline "success" stories. Sarah decides she's going to keep her four-year-old seated in the shopping cart until he can control himself in the store. Mary says that she and Steve are having an easier time with their teenage daughter ever since they started being strict about limits, like no TV before homework, and being more patient about taking time to talk to her—especially when they disagree.

Additional Information/Resources

For more on discipline, consult the following sources:

> American Academy of Child & Adolescent Psychiatry, Discipline, No. 43; Updated November 2004.
> Link: *http://www.aacap.org/cs/root/facts_for_families/discipline*

> American Academy of Pediatrics, Committee on Psychological Aspects of Child and Family Health, "Guidance for Effective Discipline." Originally published in Pediatrics in April 1998; statement of reaffirmation published October 1, 2004.
> Link: *http://aappolicy.aappublications.org/cgi/reprint/pediatrics;101/4/723.pdf*

> The American Psychological Association. Help Center. "Parenting: The Teen Years."
> Link: *http://apahelpcenter.org/articles/article.php?id=1*

Chapter Six

Healthy Eating for Families

Katherine knows that she and her family should eat better, but there never seems to be enough time. Either she's too tired to cook and stops for carry-out on the way home or she gets home and realizes there's nothing good in the refrigerator. And every time she turns on the TV, there is another report about what people should or shouldn't eat. Like a lot of us, Katherine wonders: How can I feed my family healthy foods when we have such a busy schedule?"

You need to drive the kids to ballet class and soccer practice, and you need to complete a report for your boss by 10:00 am the next day. And you still have to decide what's for dinner.

The key to healthy eating and healthy families is knowing what nutritious foods you want your family to eat, preparing food in advance to avoid last-minute fattening choices, and gathering the family together for meal time.

Here's what you need to know about weight control and eating to stay healthy. They are not exactly the same.

Weight control

The key to weight control is calories in, calories out. Family members who want to control their weight need to eat and drink fewer calories than they burn off when they exercise, sit, and sleep every day. Calorie needs vary by age and sex, and girls and women burn off fewer calories than boys and men. Experts estimate the following calorie requirements for you and your family:

Remember, some foods like chips, donuts, and candy bars have almost no nutritional value and only add calories. If you are going to eat those foods, eat them in small quantities and don't eat them often. If you can't stop eating them once you start, try to keep them out of your house and office. Out of sight, out of mind!

Individual	Ages	Light Physical Activity	Moderate Physical Activity
Child	2–3	1,000	1,000–1,400
Female	4–8	1,200	1,400–1,600
Male	4–8	1,400	1,400–1,600
Female	9–18	1,600	1,600–2,000
Male	9–18	1,800	1,800–2,200
Female	19–30	2,000	2,000–2,200
Male	19–30	2,400	2,600–2,800
Female	31–50	1,800	2,000
Male	31–50	2,200	2,400–2,600
Female	over 50	1,600	1,800
Male	over 50	2,000	2,200–2,400

For every additional two miles of brisk walking you do each day, or equivalent exercise, you can add approximately 200 calories. For ages that are not listed, calorie requirements can be estimated from the information provided, or visit *www.nhlbi.nih.gov/health/public/heart/obesity/wecan/learn-it/balance.htm.*

Eating habits of healthy families

It's important to pay attention to what you eat. Fresh fruits and vegetables are good for everyone, and most fats should be eaten in small quantities. Avoid trans fats, which are cheap-to-produce fats that help foods that look fresher longer but are bad for your waistline and cholesterol levels. Also, try to stay clear of saturated fats—fats that come from animals (lard and dairy fat, for instance) or oils like cotton-seed oil, palm kernel oil, and coconut oil. If you cook your own meals, you control what is in them. When you are buying prepared foods or ingredients to cook your own meals, check the calories, fats, and other information on the package before you buy.

Eating out, bringing fast food home, or ordering take-out is something a lot of working families end up doing more often than they plan to. When choosing where to go, remember that restaurant meals are not necessarily better for you than fast foods. The vegetables and sauces may be made with butter, cream, or other high-fat ingredients.

Tips for Choosing What to Eat and Drink:

Here are a few helpful guidelines for you to remember:

> Chicken and fish are usually healthier than beef, but not if you fry them or prepare them with lots of butter or oil.

> Baking or grilling is healthier than frying.

> Fiber is also important: from fruits, veggies, beans, certain breads, and whole grains. If you want the benefits of fruit, eat the fruit whole instead of drinking fruit juice, which is high in calories, provides limited nutrition and almost none of the fruit's fiber. Besides keeping you "regular," fiber makes you feel fuller.

> Whole grains are better for you than "white" or "refined" flours because they have about twice the nutritional value and fiber. Sometimes food manufacturers try to put the nutrition and fiber back by "enriching" the flour, but the amount of fiber in the food will usually still be low.

> If your salad contains dressing, cheese, eggs, and/or meat or fried chicken, it may be high in calories and fat. So, if your family loves burgers, it makes more sense to occasionally eat burgers rather than loading up on fattening salads.

> Fruit drinks, soda, and alcohol are fattening, and they don't fill you up. You can keep everyone's weight down by replacing high-calorie drinks with low-calorie drinks and by avoiding large drinks. Don't forget low-fat milk or calcium-fortified juice for your kids. They are not low in calories, but the calcium is important.

> Beans are easy, inexpensive, high in protein, and low in fat and cholesterol. Pinto beans, black beans, garbanzo beans, lentils— you name it—can all be used instead of meat or can be added to a dish to give it extra protein and fiber. One idea: make chili ▶

by adding a lot of canned beans and canned tomatoes to a little ground beef or turkey. Serve it over rice with some grated low-fat cheddar cheese and you have a filling, nutritious meal.

Cooking meals the easy way

Preparing meals in advance, making shopping lists, and doing the grocery shopping on a specific day can help make cooking more manageable. Try to find time to create a few meals that are easy to warm up, or can be served cold in the summer, and that will provide a healthy alternative to fast food.

If you have easy-to-prepare foods available at home, you won't need to stop by the grocery store so often. Involve your children in shopping and food preparation to help them appreciate what they are eating. It's good for them to see you checking labels and prices, and pitching in at mealtime should be everyone's responsibility. These days there are many cookbooks written just for kids. You can let your children pick a couple of recipes and make dinner with them or let them take a turn each week making a meal all by themselves. You will probably have to stay close by to supervise but you can put your feet up or unwind in other ways while they cook. Not only will your kids learn important life skills, but they will be much more likely to try new foods if they have been involved in preparing them.

Little Tricks to Keep You and Your Family Eating Right

Every working mother has to be part magician, so be sure to keep these handy tricks up your sleeve:

> ➤ Lay down the law about snacks. No one should eat chips, cookies or anything right out of the bag because that leads to over-eating. Insist on snacks being served in certain (small) bowls and ask everyone to limit servings to one bowl.

> ➤ If you are going to make the switch from white or refined flour foods and expect resistance, go "brown" slowly. Start by ▶

switching from regular pasta to whole wheat or even pasta that has some vegetables ground into the flour, like spinach fettuccine. They taste very similar to regular pasta but have extra nutrition. Next you might try a whole wheat bread or use brown rice instead of white rice. You may find that your family likes the fuller, nuttier flavor of these whole grain foods.

> ➤ Every magician has an assistant: let vegetables be yours.
> By throwing in some frozen or fresh vegetables into a pasta dish or casserole, you can make a "one-pot" meal that is nutritious, delicious and easy to clean up. Use vegetables to add color to your meal—it will look pretty and be better for you. The more (natural) colors in a meal, the more vitamins and minerals you're getting because in nature every color carries a specific package of nutrients—for example, orange usually means a vegetable is high in Vitamin A.

> ➤ Did you know that plate sizes have gotten bigger since you were a child? If you serve your family meals or snacks on smaller plates, the servings will look bigger and your family will eat less and still feel satisfied.

For those times when you get home late or everyone is just too hungry to spend time cooking, be sure to have, in your freezer or cupboards, quick options that are low in fat. Individual frozen dinners tend to have small portions and be high in fat, salt, and calories, but there are frozen family meals that are reasonably healthy and much less expensive than fast food. Whether it's a family size frozen lasagna or chicken with pasta and vegetables, make sure you check the calories and portion sizes. Most portion sizes listed on packages are much smaller than what people typically eat. Also, if the package skimps on the veggies, you can easily add more (frozen or fresh) vegetables while you're cooking.

Putting together a family meal at the end of a long day can be challenging, so make dessert one less thing to worry about. There is no law that says that dessert needs to be a part of every meal, so consider limiting dessert to certain nights of the week or special occasions, and if everyone really craves something sweet after dinner, offer fresh fruit.

Snacks

If your family likes to snack, provide healthy choices that include fruit and low fat cheese sticks or chocolate milk. Snacks at regular times throughout the day can be part of a nutritious diet. Cookies and candy are fine in moderation—but not unlimited amounts and not every day.

Gather together for meal time

Research shows that families who eat together are usually healthier, happier families. Family meals help parents ensure that children are eating right and give them a chance to learn about their kids' lives. Teenagers who eat with their families regularly are less likely to abuse drugs or alcohol or get into trouble in other ways.[1]

Research also shows that TV and eating are a dangerous combination. Whether snacks or meals, eating while watching TV tends to cause weight gain.[2,3] One simple rule—"no one eats in front of the TV"—will help to keep your family healthier and will probably help your kids do better in school.

Katherine feels like she and her family are starting to eat a lot better now that they've introduced a few simple changes to the way they eat. It's also a big relief to not be the only one in charge of deciding on meals and preparing them. Last night they all sat down to eat a dinner the kids had helped prepare. Her children helped decide what they would eat and helped make the meal, and her son had decorated the plates with different color vegetables. The one decision Katherine has made herself: family meals are a priority. They are eating together almost every night, and that helps them catch up on each other's day and feel like a family.

Chapter

Seven

Kids, TV, and Video Games

Stephanie has her hands full after work when the kids are home and hungry for dinner. Her 10-year-old, Sara, wants to watch her favorite reality shows, which will keep her busy while Stephanie cooks dinner. Stephanie isn't sure what programs her daughter is watching, but Sara says that all her friends watch them. And besides, Stephanie figures the programs must be O.K. for children if they are on so early in the evening.

How often have you heard your child mimic a song, words, or an idea that he or she saw on television? Most children spend more time in front of the TV than in school—and it teaches them many lessons— some good, and some bad.

TV and video games can be a convenient babysitter or source of entertainment, and kids love them! So, many working moms rely on them. But like most things that are "free" or relatively inexpensive, there can be hidden costs that you need to know about.

Very young children, for instance, are affected just by being in the same room with the TV on—even if they are not watching it. A recent study found that when an adult TV program was on, babies and toddlers didn't play as intently or as long as when the TV was off.[1] Since play is one of the most important ways that young children learn, we need to be concerned about that. Two-thirds of children under six may not be learning as much as they should because they live in homes where the TV is on half the time.[2] Does that include your home?

TV can directly influence children and teens by what they see and hear, or indirectly because they are watching TV instead of spending time playing with friends, talking to family members, reading, or doing other activities.

What does TV teach your children?

Would you let a stranger come into your house and spend a few hours a day with your children without supervision? Wouldn't you want to carefully check this person out first? Letting your children watch TV programs you are not familiar with can have the same impact as letting a stranger into your house. TV programs shape children's ideas, values, opinions about other people and activities, as well as their words and behavior. The standards for the content of daytime TV programs are much different than they used to be, and cable TV programs have even looser standards because the networks point out that people are paying for—and therefore *choosing*—them. Even the programs you love can influence how your child thinks and acts in ways you might not like. Desperate housewives and know-it-all kids may say things that are funny to you, but chances are you won't be laughing when the same lines come out of your nine-year-old's mouth. Hundreds of studies conclude that kids who watch TV:

> Imitate the words, violence, sexy ideas, and taunts that they see on TV.

> Learn that violence is a way to solve problems and become numb to it.

> Identify with certain characters, some of which parents may not like.

You might wonder how studies can prove that TV influences kids. Some researchers show kids a TV program featuring a particular behavior and then watch them in daycare or school to see if they imitate it (they do!). Other researchers ask kids to keep a diary of all the programs they watch on TV and video games they play, and then ask their teachers (who don't see the diaries) which kids are bullies, which ones have behavior problems, and which ones help others.[3] The researchers then find out whether children with certain TV and video game habits tend to have problem behaviors. The research shows that children who watch violent TV shows or play violent video games are much more likely to be identified by their teachers as having problems.

When parents supervise their children's TV viewing, they can increase the good things kids learn and decrease the bad things. That is one reason why you should watch TV with your kids when possible, and why kids should watch TV in a room that you or other adults spend a lot of time in. TVs do not belong in children's bedrooms—no matter how old your children are. It is very hard to control what your child watches and for how long—something all parents should be interested in doing—if the TV is in a child's bedroom.

How to reduce the bad lessons from TV and video games

Watching TV and playing video games with your children is the perfect time to talk about what they are seeing and learning. You can cuddle while watching a favorite program and then discuss what you like or don't like about the show during commercials or after it's over. Ask questions. Find out how much they understand of what they are watching and what their impressions are of the characters—especially the decisions they make and how they act.

If your child enjoys video games, you need to look at what is in each game or better yet, play it at least once. Video games have ratings, but you may be surprised by what the people rating them have decided is acceptable for your child's age. Also, children borrow games from friends whose parents may not be as careful as you are, and you'll find that the video games most popular with children are often not the ones rated for "Everyone" or even for "Teens." Video and computer games should be played in a "common" room where grown-ups are sure to listen or take a peek at the screen from time to time.

According to the American Academy of Pediatrics, a child who watches 3-4 hours of non-educational TV a day will "witness" 8,000 murders by the time he or she has finished elementary school.[4] Experts are even more concerned about children playing violent video games than they are about them watching TV shows or movies with violence. Children who watch a lot of TV may become numb to violence and think it is "no big deal." Violent games that encourage children to destroy an "enemy" are played over and over until the children are good at it. Video games can be educational, but the violent video games teach children to think and act aggressively— even in real life.

In one study, researchers assigned half of a group of college students to a violent video game and the other half to a non-violent game. On the third day of playing, both groups of students were told they could punish their opponent if he or she lost. The students who had been playing the violent video game punished their losing opponents more severely than those playing the non-violent video game.[5]

What about Babies and TV?

Some parents think that all young children, even infants, can learn from educational TV programs and DVDs, and some buy videos that are intended to make their babies "brainy." The American Academy of Pediatrics strongly disagrees, saying that children under two should not watch TV or videos. The good news is that parents can save some money: Recent research shows that children who watch these kinds of educational videos know fewer words than children who spend more time interacting with adults and other children.[6] That's the way infants and very young children learn best.

The Top 10 TV Tips:

1. Even educational TV is not as good as talking and playing with children. Avoid TV (videos, movies, computer games, and screens of any kind) for children under two. TV should be a last resort for babies and toddlers, not a frequent daily activity. The latest research shows that videos that promise to make your baby smarter don't. Children learn to talk by interacting with people—not machines.

2. Discourage TV viewing right before bedtime because, instead of relaxing them, it tends to make it harder for children to fall asleep. If it is a special show or movie that you want them to see, record it so you can watch it together during the daytime.

3. No TV in your child's bedroom—at any age. Children who have a TV in their bedroom spend more time watching TV programs and less time reading or playing.

4. TV should not be a substitute for reading or playing with friends or family.

5. Tie TV with reading. Kids can follow-up interesting TV programs by reading a book on the same topic, or if the program is based on a book, encourage them to read the book or other books by the same author.

6. Set consistent limits on TV and video games when your children are small, and remember that even when they are older, you're still the boss! Plan your child's TV viewing for

▶

specific programs or videos, not merely "anything that is on."
If children have a limited number of hours that they can watch
TV, and are allowed *some* choice as they get older, they will
become more selective consumers of television.

7. Watch at least one episode of a new program that your child
   wants to watch before you let him watch it. For new movies
   and video games, check out sites like
   www.commonsensemedia.org before you buy, rent or borrow
   them. Since video games are played over and over, it is still a
   good idea to play each game once with your child or stay close
   by the first time he plays it. That way you can make sure you
   are okay with the game's imaginary world, its rules and
   its goals.

8. Watch TV with your child and talk about what you see. Help
   your child to think about the characters and the content of both
   programs and commercials, and explain your own feelings and
   ideas. If your child plays video games, talk about those too.
   Discuss alternatives to violence as a way to solve problems.
   Point out positive examples and role models for your children
   and help them be comfortable with people who are different.
   If your child is watching shows with commercials, be sure that
   she understands the message "behind" the message.

9. Encourage your child to watch programs that demonstrate
   helping, caring, and cooperation. Studies show these types of
   programs can teach kids to act this way, too.

10. As your children get older and start to use computers, you will
    need to limit the total amount of time they spend on TV, videos,
    and computer games. For children older than two, the American
    Academy of Pediatrics recommends keeping "screen" time to
    two hours or less a day. Time in front of screens is time *not* spent
    moving around and burning calories. If your child loves video
    games, encourage him to play some of the newer, more
    innovative ones that involve physical activity like dancing.

What are the indirect effects of watching TV?

It is important to limit TV viewing, not just because of what children watch, but because of how it takes their time away from other activities. When our children watch hours of TV, they have less time for other important activities like reading, spending time with their friends and family, getting exercise, playing outdoors, or getting enough sleep.

Watching TV doesn't burn calories and it doesn't help children develop an imagination, which Albert Einstein said "is more important than knowledge." That's why kids who watch a lot of TV tend to have lower reading scores, are more overweight, and don't do as well in school. Even if your children are very smart, they might be even smarter (or more physically fit, or more relaxed) if they watched less TV.

Children who watch two hours of TV or more on week nights—even children as young as two—have more body fat than children who watch less TV.[7] And the more TV a child watches on week nights, the more likely she is to be overweight, have high cholesterol and smoke as an adult.[8]

Exactly why do kids who watch TV tend to be overweight? Maybe they are eating more of the sodas and fattening foods that they see advertised on TV, or maybe they are getting less exercise. Some kids like to eat snacks or meals while watching TV, which is a habit that is hard to break (so make it a rule: no eating while watching TV). And perhaps parents who give in to their children's demands to watch more TV are also more likely to give in to their children's demands for fast food and candy. Whatever the reason, if you care about your children's health, limit the number of hours they spend watching TV every day. Also, think about what other fun activities you can encourage family members to do to keep them from turning into "couch potatoes."

Stephanie realizes she should check out what her daughter Sara is watching on TV. It does not take long to figure out that her daughter's favorite reality show is not appropriate for a 10-year old. Despite cries of "but all my friends watch it," Stephanie decides to block the show and several others. She gets out her TV instruction manual and is relieved to find it is easier than she expected. Now she understands that even early evening cable TV can be very inappropriate for her children and makes it a point to watch other programs to determine whether they are good choices or should be blocked.

Additional Information/Resources

These sites can help you make decisions about which TV programs, movies, and electronic games are right for your child:

> *www.commonsensemedia.org*

> *www.kids-in-mind.com*

> *www.screenit.com*

Chapter

Eight

Tips to Keep You and Your Family Healthy

Between holding down a full-time job, carpooling her children, and preparing meals, Tamara jokes that she is too busy to get sick. But she does get sick, and so do her kids.

When her children were little, she went running to the doctor's office for every little thing. Even with health insurance, Tamara has seen how unnecessary doctor visits and medicines can chip away at her paycheck and waste hours in the doctor's waiting room. Now that her children are no longer babies, she is less likely to panic, but she wishes she knew more about preventing and treating common illnesses. Her mom has lots of advice, but Tamara isn't sure if those old-fashioned remedies are any good. How can she look after her health and the health of her children while keeping costs down?

We have all heard the expression "an ounce of prevention is worth a pound of cure." But we are bombarded by reports on TV and in magazines about new health findings, many of which seem to conflict with each other, and so it is easy to feel confused about what to believe or do. The good news is that some of the old-fashioned, low-cost remedies really work. The hard part is knowing which ones.

Some simple health do's

Do wash your hands with soap for 15 seconds after using the bathroom, after handling money—think of all the people who have touched those bills!—and at regular intervals throughout the day. (Hint: 5 seconds isn't enough no matter how much soap you use!) Teach your children to do this as well. Hand washing is the single most effective way to prevent colds and infections, and it costs almost nothing!

Do make getting enough sleep a high priority for you and your family. Treat it with the same importance you treat wearing a seat belt, because sleep is a health and safety issue. Too little sleep weakens your immune system and makes you prone to accidents.

Do get your children vaccinated. Vaccines occasionally cause problems, but they save lives—doing much more good than harm. Required vaccinations can almost always be gotten free-of-charge or at low cost. Young children and older people, especially those with asthma or other respiratory problems, should also get annual flu shots. About one in five people comes down with the flu every year and it is the sixth leading cause of death.

Do take folic acid supplements if you are a woman or over 65. Half of all pregnancies are unplanned, and developing babies need folic acid immediately after they are conceived—before a woman knows she is pregnant.[1] Without enough of this B vitamin, the baby's brain and spinal cord may not develop properly, resulting in serious birth defects. And, the latest research shows that folic acid helps older brains too, preventing memory loss. Citrus fruits and juices, leafy green vegetables, beans, peanuts, broccoli, asparagus, peas, lentils and whole-grain breads and other whole-grain foods are naturally rich in folic acid. It is in most daily vitamins and in vitamin B supplements.

Do get a little sun. Sunshine is a natural (and free) source of Vitamin D, and more than half of all women and 41% of all men don't get enough of this important vitamin. All you need is 15 minutes each day. Teenage girls who get more sun and drink more milk are less likely to develop breast cancer as adults. Vitamin D is so powerful that it helps people with cancer, heart disease and other serious illnesses survive longer. The latest research shows that even people without serious illnesses are less likely to die if they have higher levels of this Vitamin.[2]

Do use sunscreen, especially if you are going to be in the sun for more than 15 minutes or between the hours of 10:00 am and 4:00 pm, when the sun's ultraviolet rays are strongest.

Do get fresh air. Colds are not caused by cold weather or feeling cold. We get more colds in winter because we spend more time indoors—close to other people who may carry a cold virus. The average person spends 90% of his or her time indoors, where the air is usually more polluted than outdoors. The Environmental Protection Agency (EPA) estimates that up to 50% of all illness is caused by indoor air pollution like mold spores, bacteria, and chemicals that are in our furniture, paint, and rugs. So spend time outside when you can.

Do give lots of fluids to drink to an adult or child who is sick. And, check out your kitchen cabinet for handy, low-cost ways of relieving the discomfort caused by common health problems like sore throats, earaches, colds, bug bites and rashes.

Kitchen Cabinet Remedies

Let **salt** come to the rescue. It can reduce swelling and discomfort in your throat and nose. For sore throats, gargle with salt alone or salt and baking soda (1 teaspoon of salt, or 1/2 teaspoon of salt and 1/2 teaspoon of baking soda combined) stirred into one 8-ounce glass of warm water. Gargle with the full glass and do this several times a day until the sore throat is gone. If after a couple of days, you still have

▶

a sore throat, see a doctor, because it could be a strep throat. For stuffy noses, use saline spray or you can buy a Neti pot. It looks like a little ceramic "Aladdin's lamp." Put salt and water into this and give yourself a real nose and throat wash. This can bring relief to allergy sufferers or people with sinus problems.

A few drops of vegetable oil (most people use **olive oil**) can be put into the ear of a child complaining of an earache. Some parents warm it slightly, but that is not necessary. If your child wakes up in the middle of the night, these oils work almost as well as over-the-counter ear drops to equalize pressure and reduce discomfort. Earaches are more painful if the child is lying flat, so be sure to prop your child up a little when he is going to sleep and give children's pain medication as needed. Just be sure not to exceed the dose or give more often than the instructions say.

Ginger tea is good for upset stomachs or digestion problems. You can buy it in tea bags or make your own by adding 1/4 cup of fresh grated ginger root to 2 cups of water. Boil this for 2 minutes, strain, and if you want it sweet, add some honey.

Chicken soup—whether homemade or canned—has been shown to ease the symptoms of the common cold. While scientists still don't fully understand which ingredients in chicken soup have anti-inflammatory properties similar to over-the-counter medications, they believe that the chicken broth is effective and other kinds of soup are not.[3]

Baking soda has many health uses. A couple of tablespoons in your baby's bath water will make her diaper rash less bothersome, and you can combine baking soda with water to make a soothing paste that can be applied to bug bites/stings, rashes, poison ivy, and sun burns. It provides a lot of relief for just a few pennies.

White grape juice can help replace lost fluids and electrolytes (important salts and minerals) in children with mild diarrhea.

Corn starch can prevent or soothe chafed skin in areas where clothing or elastic is rubbing.

Water—Use cold water for burns and steam for stuffy noses. If you are congested and don't have asthma, spend a couple of minutes over a simmering pot of water or in a steam-filled bathroom. Be sure

▶

to sleep on your side or prop yourself up with pillows. If you have a dry cough, a humidifier near your bed can help. A cool mist humidifier is safer to use with children.

Some simple health don'ts

Don't use antibiotics for colds or the flu. About half of the 100 million antibiotic prescriptions written annually in the U.S. are unnecessary, because the person has a virus. Antibiotics do not kill viruses—only bacteria. (In addition to causing colds and the flu, viruses are the cause of most children's ear infections). Doctors know this, but tell us that patients pressure them to prescribe something, so they prescribe antibiotics. But, according to the American College of Physicians, using antibiotics too often or not finishing a prescription reduces their effectiveness and can cause antibiotic resistance.[4] This means the bacteria become stronger, so that antibiotic medicines can no longer kill them, making the bacteria so dangerous that there may be no cure.

Don't send your kids to school, daycare or other public places when they have a cold or the flu if you can avoid it. Finding last minute childcare can be a challenge, but letting your kids be with other children while sick means they may infect others and will also take longer to get well. If all parents would abide by this golden rule, all families would benefit. The same applies to you: try to stay home when you have a cold or flu.

Don't think you need antibacterial soap and antibacterial wipes. These soaps are very useful in hospitals where there are many sick people, many bacteria, including deadly ones, and many possibilities for bacteria to spread, but in your home, old fashioned soap and water will do. No one really understands why children have so many more allergies and so much more asthma now than in the past, but one theory is that kids today don't come into contact with enough dirt and bacteria. Their immune systems don't have a lot of practice recognizing and defending against bacteria so their immune systems (the body's army) gets confused and tries to fight against pollen, animal dander and other common substances as if they were enemies. Children raised on farms, who have regular contact with soil and farm animals, are much less likely to develop asthma.[5] So don't worry about keeping your home sterile—too much cleanliness can make your kids sick!

Don't give infants and young children cough or cold medicine. We want to help our children when they are sick, but over-the-counter cold medicines do not work for children. Experts tell us that children are more likely to end up in the Emergency Room from over-use of children's cold medications than they are to get better from them. Cold medications can no longer be advertised for children under two, but there is no evidence that they work for children of any age. Some can help children fall asleep, but if they have that effect they can also be dangerous. The only effective medications for children's colds are children's pain medications, which also reduce fevers. Cough and cold medications are a waste of money.

Don't take over-the-counter cold medications yourself, especially ones that have medication for symptoms you don't have. Remember that colds and the flu get better in a few days, whether or not you have any medicine. Most cold medications do not work, but if you have found one of the few that helps with a runny nose or congestion, you can take it. Just remember that it won't affect how long your illness lasts or whether you infect other people.

Don't give your child aspirin. Children under 18 should never take aspirin because of a rare but serious condition called Reyes' Syndrome, which can cause death in just a few days.

Fever do's and don'ts

To reduce fever or pain for children over 6 months, do use acetaminophen (such as Tylenol) or ibuprofen (such as Motrin and Advil) at the recommended doses. Don't use these medications for any infants under 6 months without a doctor's advice, and always figure out the dose by using your child's weight—not his or her age. For children under 3 months, consult your doctor at the first sign of fever (go to the Emergency Room if your doctor is unavailable).

Fevers can be upsetting to children and their parents, but since fever is the body's way of fighting off illness, it is sometimes best to let the fever do its job instead of fighting it with medication. Amazing as it sounds, doctors recommend that for children older than 3 months, no medication is usually needed until a child's temperature reaches 101—unless the child is very uncomfortable or has a history of seizures caused by fevers.[6] That means that a temperature of 99 or 100 is nothing to worry about if your child (over the age of 3 months) has a cold or the flu.

You know your child best, so if you have concerns or your child's fever is higher than 101, you should call your pediatrician. The nurse or doctor will want to know how your child is acting (Is he eating and drinking? Does he still seem to want to play?), and about his appearance. While fevers above 102 can sometimes be dangerous, a lot depends on your child's history, the other symptoms he has, and how he responds to fever-lowering medicine.

What You Should Have in Your House

None of these require a prescription, and most can be bought for less than $5.

> Soap. Always wash cuts and scrapes with soap and water before doing anything else.

> Acetaminophen (such as Tylenol or generic medicine) and ibuprophen (Advil or Motrin or generic medicine) for headaches, body aches, and fever. Ibuprophen is slightly better for fevers. Generic medicine, like drugstore brands, is exactly the same as brand-name medicine and should work just as well as the more expensive brand names.

> Saline nose spray to help unplug stuffy noses and keep mucous running clear.

> Saline eye drops to clean and soothe irritated eyes.

> An electrolyte solution like Pedialyte for children to drink after diarrhea, to prevent dehydration. Adults can usually be fine with water.

> Epsom salts for the bath to soothe sore or aching muscles.

> Benadryl in case of an allergic reaction.

> Hydrogen peroxide (3%) or Betadine to use on minor cuts and scrapes after washing them.

> Antibacterial ointment for better healing of wounds and blisters.

> Hydrocortisone cream for severe itching from rashes or stings. Just use a very small amount each time.

> Cotton balls, gauze pads, medical tape, and bandages of various sizes.

> Child-safe insect repellant. Remember that most insect repellants, such as those containing DEET, work by harming the insect's nervous system. Unfortunately, if you use too much, they can also affect a child's nervous system (or even an adult's nervous system).

> Sunscreen (30 SPF or higher). Unfortunately, SPF ratings are not always reliable. For safe and effective sunscreens, check out this Web site: *http://www.cosmeticsdatabase.com/special/sunscreens2008/brandranks.php*

> A mercury-free digital thermometer (you'll need a rectal one too if you have a child under 3).

> Tweezers for removing splinters, pieces of glass, and ticks.

> Sharp scissors for cutting gauze and tape.

> Rubbing alcohol for sterilizing thermometers, tweezers or other similar items.

> ➤ A hot water bottle for everything from stomachaches to earaches to feeling blue.

> ➤ Ice or an ice pack in your freezer to reduce swelling from falls, sprains and bites.

When to go to the doctor

Most of the following health problems can be handled at home but sometimes they require medical attention.

Colds, flu and sore throat

The way to tell a flu from a cold is that your entire body feels bad. A person suffering from the flu can have: a fever as high as 104, chills and shakes, headaches and body aches, and a sore throat or dry cough. The person is likely to feel very tired and may even throw up or have stomach pain.

A person sick with a virus (cold, cough or flu) usually starts to feel a little better around the third day, and by the fifth day should be on the road to recovery, although some symptoms might linger for up to two weeks. If there is a fever, it usually comes at the beginning of the illness and should not last more than 3–4 days. You generally don't have to do anything to bring down a fever unless it is over 101 or the person is extremely uncomfortable. To reduce fevers, give acetaminophen (such as Tylenol) or ibuprophen (Motrin or Advil) and apply a cold washcloth to the forehead, or have the person sit in a cool bath. For children under 1 year old, contact the doctor if the fever goes above 101 or if the feverish child has a stiff neck and is unusually sleepy, or is drooling and having difficulty breathing. Call the doctor at the first sign of fever if your baby is under 3 months old.

If after five days, the person has not gotten over the worst of the cold or flu, or the person develops a fever after the first few days of sickness, or if the mucous starts to get very thick and green, then this person may need to see a doctor. He or she could have what is called a "secondary infection," which often means some bacteria spotted a body weakened by a virus (for bacteria this is like a hotel vacancy sign!) and moved in. Infections that can follow a cold or flu include: ear infections, sinus infections and even pneumonia.

Sore throats—especially when they come on slowly and are not accompanied by a stuffy or runny nose—can be caused by bacteria called streptococcus ("strep throat"). If you suspect a sore throat is "strep throat" you will have to go to the doctor for a test and treatment.

Upset stomach or diarrhea

Stomach upset and diarrhea lasting more than a day or two may require a visit to the doctor. Diarrhea can cause dehydration, which means the body has lost too much fluid and too many electrolytes—salts and minerals the body needs to function. Children can get dehydrated much more quickly (in as little as a day) than adults, so they should be given clear broths or soups with salt in them and foods high in potassium like bananas or avocados right away, and have them drink white grape juice. Easy-to-digest foods like rice and dry toast can help fill their empty tummies.

How do you know if your child is dehydrated from diarrhea? Signs of dehydration are: no wet diapers for 3 hours or more (older children may not urinate much or their urine may be less pale than usual and look more concentrated); no tears when crying; dry mouth and tongue; high fever, no energy or overly fussy; skin that does not "bounce back" after you pinch it. The soft spot on the head, the abdomen or cheeks and eyes may look sunken in. If your child has any signs of dehydration, over-the-counter rehydration liquids are better than water or other drinks because they contain electrolytes. Examples are Pedialyte, Ceralyte or Infalyte. Also, consult with your doctor.

Even if dehydration is not a problem, you should see a doctor if you or your child: have diarrhea for more than 3 days, have diarrhea and a fever of a 102 or higher, have blood in your stool (or it looks black and tarry), or you have diarrhea along with strong pain in your abdomen or rectum.

Allergic reactions

If you have any of these signs after a sting or within a couple of hours of eating or drinking something, seek immediate medical attention:

> Shortness of breath or wheezing

> The feeling that your throat is closing

> Swelling of the face, lips, or tongue

> Redness or hives all over your body

> Nausea or vomiting

> Fever or chills

> Muscle aches and cramps

> Weakness

If you have Benadryl in your medicine cabinet, it is a good idea to take the dose recommended on the box while you are waiting to get medical attention.

Rashes, wounds or bug bites that seem to be getting worse

If a rash, wound or bug bite seems to be getting worse instead of better—it is oozing pus, is red or hot to the touch, or the area affected looks like it's growing in size—see a doctor. Bacteria like staphylococcus ("Staph infection") may have gotten into the open skin and may require treatment with antibiotics.

Tamara decided to sign up for a first aid course near her house. It's not expensive, it only takes one Saturday, and the materials include lots of useful telephone numbers like where to call in case of poisoning. A friend told her about a few reliable Web sites where she can go for health information, such as the one for the Center for Disease Control and Prevention (http://www.cdc.gov/Family/) and the American Academy of Pediatrics (http://www.aap.org/topics.html.) The other day, when her mother called with a sore throat, Tamara was the one saying "gargle with salt water."

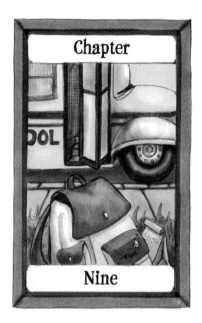

Chapter

Nine

Back to School: Getting Off on the Right Foot

While other people are making resolutions for the New Year in late December, Alison feels like the time for a fresh start is when her kids go back to school in September. There's so much to do to get ready—but it isn't just the back-to-school shopping and forms to fill out that are on Alison's mind. She wants this year to be better—homework done on time, mornings that are less frantic—and she wants to stay on top of everything instead of feeling like there is too much to do. Where should she start?

If you want to get off on the right foot, you might want to do your "spring cleaning" in the summer, after school is out, so that you can take the time to sort through papers, books, and clothes to figure out what to keep, what to get rid of, and what you need to buy for the beginning of the school year.

Out with the old

It can be hard to get kids to do their part when what they feel like doing after a busy school year is…nothing. Some parents give their kids at least a week or two to unwind before asking them to go through and organize their belongings. Others think it is better that the kids spend an hour or more a day doing these chores *before* totally relaxing or starting camp or summer jobs. Younger children will need a parent to help them. Even older children often need adult input ("It's time to throw away those old sneakers!").

In with the new

While you probably are going to wait until August to do your back-to-school shopping in case your child grows two inches over the summer, you and your child can start making a list of what he or she will need as you organize last year's stuff and get rid of clothes that have outlived their usefulness. Some schools send a mailing during the summer, letting you know when school starts and listing the items your children will need for the fall. Other schools maintain Web sites with this information. If your child is entering a new school, make sure you have a copy of the school's handbook, as it may tell you what your child should bring on the first day or describe the dress code. Dress codes can be a life-saver when it comes time to buy back-to-school clothes. If your child's ideal school wardrobe conflicts with your ideas of what he or she should wear to school, you may be able to simply say, "Sorry, the dress code doesn't allow that."

When it is time to shop for new clothes, school uniforms and school supplies, don't forget to include safety equipment for sports, if necessary. Not all schools supply mouth guards or pads for knees, shins and wrists.

Staying on top of all the forms

If your children are not automatically re-enrolled or they are entering a new school, before turning your attention to medical and emergency contact forms, make sure your kids are actually enrolled and that any fees due at the time of enrollment are paid!

Once you are sure of this, your next task may be to schedule a doctor's visit. A lot of families schedule their children's annual check-up toward the end of the school year or during the summer. This way, they can make sure kids get the immunizations required for the next school year and can give their doctor the school or state health forms that need to be filled out. Also, if your child must take medicine while at school—for asthma or any other recurring or chronic health problem—your doctor may need to fill out a form for the school with instructions or a form that gives the child permission to carry and take the medicine during the school day.

The annual check-up is a great time to discuss with your pediatrician how to keep your child healthy during the school year. Colds, stomach flu, ear infections, pink eye (conjunctivitis) and sore throats are the top reasons kids miss school, so ask your child's doctor how to spot and treat these health problems if you are not sure.

Getting ready for the school year: Dress rehearsals

The slower days of summer offer a great opportunity to fine-tune some of the daily tasks you and your family need to do during the school year, like fixing snacks and packing lunch to take to school. Even if your children's school provides lunch, your child may have dietary restrictions, health concerns, or simply does not like what is being served on certain days. Many parents pack meals in a hurry or with no participation from their children—only to have the lunch box return home at the end of the day with uneaten, spoiled food. Or, the kids are in charge and the lunch box is full of unhealthy foods. What you can do during the summer is come up with guidelines for packing lunches and snacks and have your kids create sample menus. If they are going to summer school, on trips, or to day camp, let them test out their menus and pack the lunches themselves—either the night before or in the morning. By the fall, you and your kids will have reached some happy compromises, and you might even find you have one less job to do each day.

The next thing you will want your children to practice as the school year approaches is going to bed earlier and getting up earlier. Bedtimes often shift quite a bit during the long days of summer, but a week or two before the first day of school you need to make sure your kids go to bed a little earlier each night. For instance, if during the school year they are in bed by 9:00 pm but they have been going to bed at 10:30 pm during the summer, have them start their bedtime routine 15 minutes earlier each night. If they have been getting up around 9:00 am during the summer, you will have to start by waking them (or setting several alarms) 15 minutes earlier each day. If you don't retrain their sleep habits, they will have a very tired first day and risk being half-asleep their whole first week of school when new rules and homework assignments are announced.

A couple of days before school starts, and after you have done some of your back-to-school shopping, have your children pick out what they are going to wear for their first (and even second day) of school. Children are often excited and even nervous about going back to school. They may want to send a message that they are the same but also older and a little different, which may mean showing off a new look. Maybe you can remember what it was like—seeing all your old friends again, some of whom you had not seen for months. The time your children would have spent fussing over what to wear will be better spent having a relaxed and nutritious breakfast on the first day.

New school year resolutions

If one of your new school year's resolutions is for your kids to eat better breakfasts, make sure that the choices available to them are healthy ones, especially when your children are fixing their own breakfast. If you don't want them to start the day with a pastry or sugary cereal, don't stock up on those things. But, be sure to check the nutrition information on the package before you buy the food, because cereals and breakfast bars that sound nutritious are often high in calories and may be less nutritious than fortified children's cereals.

If you are the one preparing breakfast, avoid offering more than two choices. You are not running a restaurant. You have to get dressed and get out the door, too! If you have pre-school or early elementary school age children, think about adopting a weekly menu that eliminates choice and gives everyone in the family a nutritious start each day. For example, Monday is scrambled eggs and toast, Tuesday is cold cereal, Wednesday is yogurt and fruit, Thursday is oatmeal, and so on. Children thrive on predictability and routine, which also makes your life easier.

Communication About School

With your children: Before the first day of school, make sure your child knows his address and any phone numbers he might need. Even preschoolers can memorize this information. If your child is nervous about starting school or about something that is going on there, socially or academically, listen to him and let him know other kids are probably going through the same thing. Never laugh at your child's fears or call them silly. Help your child find strategies for dealing with his fears or difficult situations and focus on the positive. Do detective work: figure out what parts of school excite your child, get him talking, and ask him about those when you first see him, instead of asking, "How was your day?"

With teachers and administrators at the school: Find out the best way to communicate with your child's teacher right from the start. Some prefer drop-off time, while others like to get a phone call, note or an email. Longer conversations about more than one aspect of your child's performance or behavior usually require a scheduled meeting. Make sure you have the phone number or Web site address needed to check on school closings and report your child's absence. Check with administrators about how they handle any late arrivals and early pick-ups. Many schools want to be notified about how your child will get home and who has permission to pick up your child.

▶

With family members, friends, and other parents at the school:
All parents, but especially working ones, need a village to help them
raise their children and make sure they get to and from school and
after-school activities safely. Talk to these "villagers" to determine
their availability and willingness to help you. Post their contact information in the house and keep it with you at all times. Discuss with
them and your kids what to do in an emergency.

If your children's school doesn't schedule regular parent nights,
you may want to meet informally with the parents of your children's
classmates to find out more about what goes on at school. Parents
whose kids are not big talkers can sometimes learn a lot by speaking
with other parents. It's also a great way to share solutions to common
problems and even make agreed-upon limits about certain behaviors
like dating or internet use. That way, when your kid says "But everyone else's parents let them," you'll know if that is true or not.

Getting your children (and their books) to school and back

Another item on your shopping list is likely to be a backpack…again.
Backpacks seem to get bulkier and heavier every year, so it's no wonder
they wear out—the zippers stop working and they rip. Invest in a good
backpack with wide shoulder straps and lots of compartments so that
the weight is better distributed and the contents can be organized.
It also helps if the part that is against your child's back is padded.
Health experts advise that backpacks should not weigh more than
10% to 20% of your child's weight. So if your daughter weighs 90 lbs.,
her backpack should not weigh more than 18 lbs.! Tell your children
to wear both straps, and if they insist on carrying the backpack over
one shoulder, switch to a backpack with wheels so that the weight is
mostly rolled instead of carried.

Figuring out how your child is going to get to school each day—
with or without books—is often a parent's number one headache.
No matter what kind of transportation your child will be using,
you need to review safety rules at the beginning of each school year.
If your child will be getting home before an adult or if he or she will be

walking, riding a bike, or taking public transportation, these discussions should also include some "what if" scenarios and role playing to make sure your child understands your advice. Many kids take cell phones to school, which can help parents feel less worried, but are not a substitute for teaching your kids basic precautions and common sense.

Tips for Traveling To and From School Safely

By school bus:

> Kids need to look both ways before crossing the street—before boarding the bus and after getting off.

> They must wait on the curb for the bus to make a complete stop.

> When on the bus, they should not move around and they should use seat belts if available.

> Remind your children that you have trouble driving when they are shouting, and their bus driver feels the same way. With so many kids in one vehicle, bus drivers especially need for children to use quiet voices.

By car:

> Preschoolers and elementary school age children traveling by car should use correctly installed car seats or booster seats. Your child should use a car safety seat with a full harness until the seat is outgrown, which is usually at about 40 lbs. Then it's time for a booster seat. An adult seat belt by itself (without a booster seat) probably will not provide a safe fit until your child is about 4'9" tall and weighs 80 lbs.

> Children under 13 should always ride in the backseat. If someone younger must ride in the front because space is limited, turn the air bag off (some cars have this feature), use a booster seat if necessary, and move the front seat as far back as you can.

> If the driver is a teenager, limit the number of passengers and tell the driver no cell phone cell use (that includes texting), eating, drinking or fiddling with music while driving. If the radio station needs changing or a call has to be made, let one of the passengers do it.

By bike:

> Children should always wear a helmet to prevent serious head injuries.

> Children can wear a bright vest or attach a tall flag to the back of the bike so drivers can see them better.

> Children should use bike lanes and trails wherever possible rather than city streets.

> Children should be taught to ride in the direction of the traffic, signal turns, and stop at lights and stop signs just as if the bike were a car.

> If your child is young and only going a few blocks, check if your town or city allows biking on the sidewalk.

Walking or taking public transportation:

> Have your child go with an adult, friend, or group of friends.

> Plan the route together and decide on places your child can wait safely in case the weather changes suddenly or if he wants to "check in" with some adults.

> Make sure, whenever possible, your child is crossing streets where there is a crossing guard, stop light, or stop sign.

> Urge your child to stand with friends or other people while waiting for a bus or subway.

> Let him know that when he is walking alone, he should always take the busiest, best-lighted routes possible.

> ➤ Remind your children that listening to music on earphones could make them unaware of danger, so they should only do that when inside buses, subway cars, or in places where there are many other pedestrians and passengers around.

Back to After-School

Getting your child off to school the first day is, of course, only half the battle. You also have to plan how and where your child will spend her time after school each day. The American Academy of Pediatrics recommends that even pre-teens (11- and 12-year-olds) should not be allowed to spend time at home alone and unsupervised after school unless they are unusually grown-up and responsible.[1] Make sure your kids have a good after-school routine that includes some "down time" but also plenty of time for homework and chores. If they will be in an after-school program, choose one that includes a quiet place to get homework done, with staff who are able to help your child if he or she has questions. Meet as a family to see if you need to make changes to last year's routine and whether there are after-school activities you want to add or drop, depending on your budget, transportation needs, and your child's interests and ability to juggle homework and extracurricular activities.

Be clear before the school year starts about your expectations about homework. If it needs to get done before your child plays, watches television or spends time socializing on the computer, let him know. And lay down ground rules about where your child does his homework, and which distracting media, if any, he can listen to or watch while doing it (HINT: homework takes longer and is more likely to have errors if done while watching TV, listening to music, etc.). Homework should be done somewhere comfortable (but not too comfortable!) that is set up for that purpose with the right supplies handy. If homework is almost always done in this place, then every time your child sits down there, he will automatically go into "homework mode." This means less nagging and less time wasted. Your role as a parent is to oversee but not do homework. If your child needs help that you are unable to give, find out if your child's school offers free or low-cost tutoring. Don't wait for a small problem to become a big one.

It's the first day of school and Alison has just left her children at the school bus stop. It took a lot of planning, shopping, and talking to get ready for this day. And it went remarkably smoothly. Alison smiles to herself, thinking, "This is going to be a good year."

Chapter

Ten

Kids and the Internet

When Anne babysits for her grandchildren, she can't believe how much time they spend on the computer. She doesn't see the attraction of most of what they do online—instant messaging, Facebook, downloading music. And, it's hard for her to tell when they are doing homework and when they are just goofing off. Anne feels like it's cutting into family time, and time that she would like to spend with them. They aren't doing things together like playing board games and baking cookies like she had done with her kids. But what can she do? This is the way it is now with kids, right?

Most of us know how emails, work and games on the computer can swallow us whole. Sometimes hours go by and you can't quite figure out how that happened. So it's no wonder that kids get glued to the computer, and that they are less able to manage their time and set priorities. And, while parents have come to expect their kids to spend hours on the computer, whether they like it or not, grandparents may be shocked—and rightfully so.

Too much of a good thing

The Internet is a wonderful tool for learning—bringing the world to our kids' fingertips, with answers to their questions only a click away. But our children don't only have access to the information that you want them to have. They also can read, view, and hear disturbing things, as well as have contact with people they don't know and who may not be who they say they are. Even when the Internet is used wisely and safely, there can be too much of a good thing. Spending a lot of time on the computer is time *not* spent on other things like doing homework, building face-to-face friendships, playing sports, reading for pleasure, or helping out around the house. It's important for parents and grandparents to understand the Internet's risks and how to minimize them.

Caution: children surfing

Most of us, at one time or other, have been bothered by a "pop-up" ad with sex-related words or images. You keep trying to close it but it keeps coming back. Or maybe you were thinking about shopping for a doll online, and after doing a search, find you are visiting a porn site that features a very different kind of "doll." If it's happened to you, you can be sure it will happen to your child.

Blocks and filters

While there are filters and blocks you can and should use, they are not 100% effective. The people who design inappropriate content are always thinking of new ways to get around blocks and filters, and new ways to link Internet users to their sites.

Filters are particularly useful for younger kids (10 and under). Parents can turn on the filtering option in their Web search engine. Parental controls or filtering options are available, for instance, with Google (Safe Search), AOL (Search Safe), Yahoo, and Windows Live. Check with your Internet service provider to see what tools it offers for filtering content and protecting your children.

You can also buy special software to block or limit what your kids are exposed to on the Internet. Programs that get good reviews include CyberPatrol, Safe Eyes, and Net Nanny. For more information, visit *www.internet-filter-review.toptenreviews.com.*

Unwanted visitors

According to Dr. David Finkelhor, Director of the Crimes Against Children Research Center, their national survey found that "1 out of 7 young people who use the Internet receive an unwanted sexual solicitation or inquiry from someone online."[1] He estimates that 1 in 25 kids is aggressively solicited, meaning the person tries to contact the child by phone or meet her. Parents need to talk to their kids about this danger, and make sure that they understand that not everyone is who he seems to be online.

Teens at risk

Teenagers are especially likely to get involved in online conversations that they can't control. Dr. Patricia Greenfield, a psychology professor at UCLA, has studied chat rooms for teens and reported that she found explicit sexual exchanges, joking about physical violence and assaults, aggression, and disturbing exchanges involving racial prejudice. Even as a passive bystander that did not participate in the "chats," she received several instant messages making sexual advances. Chat rooms that were not monitored were especially worrisome, but even those that were monitored were not always successful at censoring that kind of material. For example, she learned that teens used codes such as "A/S/L" (age, sex, location) to provide information that would not have been allowed. And, although the chat rooms were supposed to be for teens, there was no way to know how young or old anyone really was.

Good Web Sites to Find Out More about Filters, Blocks and Internet Safety

> If you are not sure which filters to choose or how to use them, go to *www.kids.getnetwise.org* and go to "Tools for Families." There you will find a checklist that can help you pick the tools you want for the computer you have.

> Another good resource is *www.safekids.com*, which has "a family's tech first-aid kit." There is a companion Web site called *www.safeteens.com* that parents of children over 10 might want to look at.

> Two good sites on how to keep your kids safe while using the Internet are *www.internetsafey.net* and *www.connectsafely.org*. The second one includes videos and discussion groups for parents.

> Children of all ages should read the one-page "Internet Survival Tips for Kids and Teens" found at the *commonsensemedia.org* Web site. Go to: *http://www.commonsense.com/internet-safety-tips/tips-for-kids.php*. Print and post this wherever your child uses the computer.

Online bullying

The ability to hide who you are also makes the Internet a safe place for bullies. Unlike online sexual predators, who tend to be older, white males with full-time jobs, online bullying is often done to kids by kids. Bullying isn't new; what's new is that the schoolyard has been replaced by cyberspace. Unlike bullying on the playground, it is easy for online bullying to happen with no adults ever knowing about it.

Other things to do to make sure your kids are safe and civil online

Filters and blocks are not enough to keep your kids safe online. Many chat rooms and other social networking sites have a minimum age requirement, but that doesn't work if children simply lie about their age. Think of these precautions as being like hand-holding. When our children are young, we can hold their hand everywhere they go, but as they get older that is no longer possible. So, we tell our children to cross at the light, but we also teach them to look both ways before crossing. We have to teach our kids how to navigate the Internet safely and appropriately, just the way we teach them how to behave on the streets and in social situations.

Guard personal information

We tell our kids not to talk to strangers, not to get into cars with people they don't know, and to kick and scream if someone tries to grab them. The problem with the Internet is that complete strangers can seem less threatening than in real life. A stranger may tell your child that they have a friend in common or pretend to be a kid your child's age. So make sure your kids know to never reveal any personal information like their complete name, address or phone number to Internet acquaintances (they should steer clear of questionnaires that ask for this information, too). When they sign into an online game, they should never give their email address or password to anyone.

Safety do's and don'ts

Tell them to discontinue contact with anyone who makes sexual remarks, sends sexual photos or other attachments, or acts like a bully. And most importantly, encourage your children to turn to you when something like this occurs, or whenever they have an interaction or receive a message they have doubts about. Assure them you won't give them the third degree; you'll just listen and help them come up with a solution, which may include alerting the Internet service provider or the game company.

Kids receive a lot of silly forwarded messages but they also can get frightening chain mail, warning that bad things will happen to them if they don't forward the message. Let them know that while we grown-ups may sometimes seem clueless when it comes to computers and the Internet, we know how to handle most situations that are troubling or new to kids.

Lastly, the golden rule still applies—even in cyberspace: Your kids should treat people online as they would want to be treated, and *never* say or do anything to someone online that they wouldn't say or do in person.

Online homework help: using a critical eye

Of course, the Internet can also be a wonderful source of information to help with homework. Your children probably will need your help figuring out which sites are good sources of information and which ones are not.

For example, Wikipedia.com, a free online encyclopedia, has become one of the most popular Web sites on the Internet. However, it is not the most accurate. Anyone with access to the Internet can edit the articles on Wikipedia, and although scholars and experts often help write articles, so do teenagers and others who may not be the most accurate or unbiased sources of information.

Tell your children to judge Internet sites a little bit like they do people. Some friends you can count on, others are always late or exaggerate, and then there are people you wouldn't befriend even if you were stranded together on a deserted island. Use a topic you know—like something from sports or a hobby you enjoy—to show your children examples of sites that give credible information on that subject, sites that are only so-so, and sites that are downright wrong. A lot of the time you can get an idea of how reliable a site is just by looking at the web address. Train your kids to look for signs that the site is about selling or marketing a product or an idea. If that is the main purpose, then the information may be slanted a particular way.

Beware of cutting and pasting

If a teenager is writing a paper for school, it is so easy to cut and paste sentences and even entire paragraphs from a Web site. That is called plagiarism. Explain to your children that they can use the ideas and information on the Internet, but that they can't use the exact words. And, if they are old enough to be using references in their papers, then they need to use references whether their information comes from a book or the Internet.

Other types of cheating

The Internet is also a source of more blatant cheating: kids can buy papers to use for school. Make sure that your child understands that buying somebody else's work and pretending it is their own is cheating.

Web Sites for Homework Help

Here are a few free sites that can provide help with homework for K-12:

All Subjects: *http://www.factmonster.com/homework/*

Math: *http://school.discoveryeducation.com/homeworkhelp/*

English: *http://school.discoveryeducation.com/homeworkhelp/ english/english_homework_help.html*

Science: *http://school.discoveryeducation.com/homeworkhelp/ science/science_homework_help.html*

Science and Geography: *http://kids.nationalgeographic.com/*

Social Studies: *http://school.discoveryeducation.com/homework-help/socialstudies/social_studies_homework_help.html*

U.S. history and Social Studies: *http://www.kids.gov/*

▶

Internet sources of information for more advanced students:
http://www.ipl.org/

Tips for Helping Your Kids Use the Internet Wisely:

Make rules about homework and the Internet. Make sure that having fun on the computer doesn't come before homework. A lot of kids think they can multi-task—doing homework with music and the TV on, while responding to a steady stream of instant messages (IM). IMs and "pings" from social networking sites alerting them of a new post can be very disruptive. Your child should turn notifications off during homework. If your child protests, you can tell him that his choice is that or removing the program from the computer.

Set time limits. Games, social networking sites like Facebook and MySpace, blogging, and YouTube can keep your child from finishing homework, keep her up late, and prevent her from being involved in other activities. The American Academy of Pediatrics recommends no more than 2 hours of screen time a day—whether it's a TV, a computer or watching a movie on an iPod.[2]

Keep an eye on things. It is better to keep the computer your children use in a common area where you can occasionally look at the screen while they are online, and can easily review the browser's history, telling you what sites they visited after they get off. Eventually, your children will learn to delete the history but until then, use this tool!

Right to know. You paid for the computer; you pay for the Internet service. It is your right to know what accounts are being set up. Younger children need to ask or at least tell you every time they set up an email account or a "page" or download anything that isn't just an upgrade to something already on the computer. As your child gets older and you are confident of his choices, you can relax these rules.

There are no secrets on the Internet. Whatever accounts or "pages" they set up, your kids need to understand the importance of using privacy settings. They should always choose "for friends only" instead of allowing wider access. They may understand not to give personal information to someone asking for it, but then post intimate

▶

details of their life on a social networking site. Tell them to assume that whatever they post will somehow, someday be seen by everyone—including college admissions, possible employers, parents of dates, etc.

Spyware and Viruses. Explain that if they click one pop-up, they will get a lot more, and that can result in viruses and spyware, too. Everyone in the family needs to help protect the computer from viruses, spyware and adware by making sure all of those programs are updated regularly and always in-use. Otherwise, viruses and spyware can make a computer unusable, and the cost of a repair can be very expensive. Free music downloads and peer-to-peer file sharing are very appealing to kids, but they need to know that there are risks. In some cases, file sharing is illegal (where copyrights are infringed) and peer-to-peer networks have been used to gain access to people's computers and steal their identity.

The charge card holder is in charge. If your child wants to buy things online or download software, music or movies that require using a charge card, you should be in charge! Either establish a budget and teach safe online shopping or provide the credit card information for each purchase yourself.

Anne spoke to several parents and grandparents, visited a couple of Web sites they told her about, and realized her instincts were right: her grandchildren were spending way too much time on the computer. She recognizes that things are different now from when her kids were growing up. But she also knows that having everybody off in separate rooms, staring at a screen, isn't good for a family. She talked to her kids and grandchildren about what was worrying her. It turned out that her older grandchildren were surprisingly well-informed about Internet safety, such as what information shouldn't be shared. Last weekend the whole family went to a baseball game together, and tonight Anne's oldest grandson has promised to show her how Facebook works.

Chapter

Eleven

Finding Time for Yourself (and Your Special Other) in a Hectic World

Time to herself? The last time Nancy can remember having time alone was when she was in bed with the flu. Between the demands of her job, two young kids, and keeping the house up and running, she hasn't even had time for a haircut in six months. And forget about romance. It's been ages since she and her husband, Eric, have been out alone.

When was the last time you went to the movies with a friend, took a class, got a pedicure, read a good book, or bought yourself some flowers? Women seem hard-wired to take care of others and often struggle with feelings of guilt when they do something for themselves. But the old saying, "If Mama ain't happy, ain't nobody happy," reminds us that we must first take care of ourselves if we want to be there for others. How can you give to your boss, your family or your friends if you are "running on empty?" Making time for yourself and for your husband or significant other is essential for your physical and mental health. In fact, a study found that 65% of women who describe themselves as "very happy" are careful to make time for themselves.[1]

Start small. Think back to activities you've enjoyed over the years. Commit to doing one activity a week for the next month. Forget lofty goals. Start with little things—sit down for a cup of tea, take a stroll, or skim through your favorite magazine. These pleasurable breaks will soon become habit and you can move onto bigger gifts for yourself.

Observe your habits. Keep a diary of your activities for a month to see where you can save time on things that are not important and fit in additional time for yourself. Perhaps you are making multiple trips to the grocery store or there are activities you can do back to back to save time. Make a wish list of things you long to do, but don't have time for. Making time for the things you really want to do will make you more efficient overall. Skimping on these activities can rob you of motivation and lead to frustration and procrastination. The following are time-saving tips to help you carve out time for Number One—you.

Time management tips for "Number One"

Just say no. If you want to learn how to say "yes" to more things that fulfill or relax you, you will first have to practice saying "no." You can't be all things to all people. It's okay to put your foot down once in a while. Break the cycle of being a constant people pleaser.

Me dates. Block off time in your schedule for things you'd like to or need to do and make them non-negotiable.

Teamwork. Trade off with other parents on carpooling, childcare and other activities. If you take your children and a friend's children to the zoo one Saturday, your friend may be able to organize an outing the following Saturday, giving you some much needed time to yourself.

Take public transportation. Take the bus or other public transportation to work. It provides time to read and relax, and to do other things you could never do while driving. If you live close enough, you could also try walking to work for some exercise and time to think.

Avoid peak times. Save time by avoiding the busiest times for your errands, such as the bank on Friday afternoon and the grocery store after work. Most grocery stores are like ghost towns after 8:30 pm.

Consolidate. Many retailers are geared toward the working parent, with a dry-cleaners, pharmacy, bank, and grocery store all near each other. That can save on time and gasoline. You can also be creative with your time: Try using your lunch hour for a quick visit to the gym or to get a manicure. The exercise can give you an extra jolt of energy and the pampering can give you the calm you need to deal with a difficult boss.

At your service. Consider using services such as online grocery shopping where groceries are delivered to your door. (Google "grocery delivery" and your city to find a delivery service near you.) House-cleaning and errand services are also big time savers. They can save enough time that the cost is worth it—especially if you don't need to buy carryout dinners as often. Visit *http://www.myerrandservice.com/directory* for an errand service in your area. Or consider hiring your kids for errands they are old enough to do.

Think ahead. Set aside time on the weekend to prep for weekly meals. Chop vegetables for salads and snacks, grill some chicken and slice it for sandwiches or salads, make recipes that can easily be frozen into meal-size containers, such as chili or casseroles.

Chill. Take five minutes for yourself as soon as you get up in the morning and before you go to bed. Find a quiet place where you will not be disturbed. It's the perfect time to meditate, write in a journal, or take in the sunrise/sunset.

Lose the perfectionism. Know when a task is done well enough. Simple meals can be just as healthy and enjoyable as complicated ones, for example.

Rely on a babysitter. You should not feel guilty about asking your spouse, family member, or friend to watch your kids. Or, find a neighborhood babysitter. Remember, nurturing yourself is critical to nurturing your child. Research shows that very young babies reflect the emotions of their caregivers. So a happier you means a happier baby.[2]

Hang the "Do Not Disturb" sign. If you have to finish something, let your co-workers or kids know that you need to focus and would like some time alone. According to a 2004 study, office workers are interrupted every three minutes on average, and once interrupted, it takes a full 25 minutes for them to return to what they were working on![3]

Delegate. You can still be Supermom, even if you have to ask your spouse or kids to pitch in. You may be on the receiving end of momentary eye-rolling, but even something as simple as your 10-year-old vacuuming or unloading the dishwasher can buy you a little time for relaxation.

Keep the romance alive

Just as it is important to find time in your day for you, it is equally important to nurture your relationship with your spouse or significant other. Staying connected and keeping the romance alive through the stresses of everyday living is a challenge we sometimes overlook. A happy marriage also benefits your children. Here are a few suggestions for keeping the spark alive:

Schedule at least one hour a week of alone time and make this an appointment that can't be broken! You need this time alone for catching up and checking in. You have heard it a million times before: communication is key to a solid marriage. This gets repeated a lot, because in this hectic, multi-tasking world we live in, it is easy for spending-time-with-your-partner to drop to the bottom of the to-do list. You need this time to make plans together, resolve differences or just share what's on your mind. Try to schedule this time during the days when you aren't tired from work. Turn off your cell phones, close the door or take a stroll and let the words come. Discussing problems or concerns as they happen will keep them from getting out of control. Remember to jot down things you wish to discuss so you don't forget.

Schedule dates with your spouse or partner. A night at the movies, a romantic dinner or late night snack, tickets to a concert or sports event—whatever your idea of a good time is, make sure you schedule fun time for just the two of you at least twice a month. Avoid unpleasant conversations, like about bills, on those special nights. This time is as important as the work you do or anything else in your day, so resist the temptation to cancel this time together, no matter what "emergency" comes up. If you can't find time in the evening or can't find a babysitter, consider having lunch together during the week or watching a movie together at home when the kids are asleep.

Stormy weather. Revisit your childhood by playing make-believe: Pretend a storm has hit and the electricity is off. Light a candle and enjoy each other's company without the TV, computer, or any other distractions.

Roll up your sleeves together. Share household chores on the weekends. Not only will they get done faster, giving you more free time to pursue your individual interests or go on family outings, but you'll get to be together and talk to each other while gardening, running errands, or repairing things in the house.

Time For Yourself: Priceless

Try finding 15–30 minutes a day to indulge yourself. Odds are it will not bring your fast-spinning world to a halt, but it will breathe fresh air into your normal routine.

> Before bed, read a few pages of a magazine or book you enjoy. If you are too tired then, try doing this right after the kids go to bed.

> Buy yourself flowers or pick some and arrange them yourself. Place the flowers—cut or in pots—by your bed or desk.

> Make a lunch date with a friend you haven't seen for awhile. If he or she lives far away, plan a weekly or monthly "phone date."

> Research something fun online like a vacation or a class you've always wanted to take.

> Enjoy a guilty pleasure, like browsing the tabloids (you can shake your head in disbelief and be grateful you don't have those problems!).

> Take a bubble bath instead of a shower.

> Walk to work.

> Window shop.

> Take a cat nap (naps of less than half an hour have been shown to increase productivity).

> Have a relaxing cup of herbal tea.

> Watch the sunset/sunrise while you stretch or do neck rolls.

> Garden or tend to your potted plants.

> Get a manicure or pedicure, or give yourself one.

> Listen to your favorite music.

Who knew? Since scheduling her time to include at least a few minutes each day for herself, Nancy feels more energized and better able to tackle the challenges of the day. She and Eric go out on a Saturday night at least once a month, and on other weekends they find a movie to watch together at home. Those few hours a week of R & R really make a difference.

Chapter

Twelve

Caring for an Aging Parent

Lori has just finished putting away the dinner dishes and helping the kids with their homework. She'd love to sit down and unwind, but now she has to begin her second shift, which involves driving to her father's house to care for him. Her 78-year-old dad recently fell and is feeling fragile and anxious. His memory also seems to be failing and he needs help with even routine tasks. Lori has been thinking that perhaps he would be better off living with her or in assisted-living housing, but he is adamantly opposed to either of these ideas. She adores her dad and wants to respect his independence, but she also wants him to be safe.

Lori's situation is similar to millions of women and men across the country. She belongs to the "sandwich generation," which means she is sandwiched between caring for an elderly or sick parent and raising children. One-third of women between the ages of 45 and 56 provide help and support on a regular basis to both parents and children, and nearly one in ten spends a lot of time each day juggling the needs of an older relative with those of their kids.[1]

Parents can be healthy and fully functioning despite their advanced years, and suddenly everything can change. Sometimes, the decline is caused by a fall, a stroke, or other serious illness. Or, for reasons that aren't obvious, a senior can suddenly have trouble taking care of himself or keeping track of what is going on in the world. Loss of memory is not necessarily a sign of Alzheimer's disease, but regardless of the cause of memory loss, it is upsetting for the person and for their loved ones.

Witnessing your parent's decline or dealing with your parent's depression following a serious illness or the death of a spouse can make even the most competent person feel helpless. Caring for an aging or ailing parent while working (and especially if you are also raising kids) is perhaps the toughest job you'll ever have. And it is a job no one applies for.

Aging is inevitable, but there are strategies that can help keep older people as healthy as possible, and can help you cope with the challenges of helping your aging parents.

An ounce of prevention: worth more than a pound of cure

You may be able to help your parents stay healthy and independent by helping them make their current living environment as safe as possible. Taking a careful look at their home and how they live will help you figure out ways to prevent accidents.

Preventing Falls

About one out of three people over the age of 65 falls each year, and falls are the leading cause of injury for older people. Forty percent of seniors who fracture their hip will end up in a nursing home and 20 percent will die within a year.[2] Hip fractures are so debilitating because older bones take longer to heal, and bed rest and reduced activity can lead to other physical and emotional ailments.

At least half of all falls among older people happen at home—often because the person was doing something beyond her abilities, in surroundings that were not safe for an older person. You can cut the likelihood of your parent slipping and falling if you make changes to their home and lifestyle, including:

> Take your parent shoe shopping. Get low-heeled or flat footwear that isn't too heavy and has good soles with traction. Slippers and socks for the house should also be non-slip.

> Put away throw rugs or small area rugs. Compared to wall-to-wall carpeting, or large rugs that fill a room, the edge of a smaller rug can easily trip up an older person. Large rugs that are kept in place by heavy furniture and with edges near the wall are safer than small rugs. Getting rid of rugs can be even better than a miracle cure for broken bones because it will prevent the falls that can cause hip fractures. If you must keep small area rugs, make sure they have rubberized backings, use a non-slip pad beneath the rug, and, if possible, tape the edges to the floor.

> Bathrooms are another spot where it is easy to take a tumble. Bath mats should be rubberized underneath and showers and tubs should have non-slip stickers or mats. Invest in products to make the bathroom safer and easier to use—grab rails in the shower, toilet seat handrails and raised toilet seats.

> Eliminate clutter, things on the floor or anything that can turn the home into an obstacle course. Cable wires and electrical cords should be minimized, bundled and secured.

▶

> ➤ Let there be light! Open the curtains or get translucent window shades and install extra lighting, including night lights. Failing eyesight together with dimly lit surroundings is a recipe for a fall. Make sure your parent gets regular eye exams and has glasses that are easily accessible at all times (neck chains are one solution).

> ➤ If your parents can't move to a home without stairs, make sure steps have non-slip treads, are well lit or have visibility strips.

How diet and exercise affects health and memory

There is no magic pill to prevent memory loss. Short term memory—what you did yesterday or even what you ate this morning—tends to deteriorate first. The good news is that there are things people can do to help stay healthy physically and mentally throughout their lives.

Eating right and moderate exercise, like walking, can really make a difference in the way an older person feels and thinks. Walking and other regular physical exercise reduce stress and can help regulate blood pressure. And the latest research shows that exercise can make older people think more clearly and improve their memory.[3] Another great way to build memory "muscles" and keep the mind limber is to do crossword puzzles, Sudoku and other thinking games.

Folic acid—a B vitamin found in leafy greens like spinach and in fortified breads and cereals—is also connected to memory. If there is any chance that your parents might not be getting enough in their diet, most daily vitamin pills will easily solve the problem. People who have too little of this vitamin are more likely to have heart disease and confused thinking. A recent study found that men and women between the ages of 50 and 70 who took double the daily recommended dose of folic acid had better memories.[4]

If your parents need your help

When serious illness strikes, or when parents become increasingly reliant on you, it's normal to wonder how you'll manage. How will you keep everything afloat? How do you deal with all the feelings you may have as your roles are reversed, with you now "parenting" your parent? How will you carve out time for yourself in an already overflowing schedule?

There are many decisions to be made, decisions that can affect the entire family. It can help if you think about your parents' health and housing needs ahead of time and start making plans before a crisis hits. You will need to have several frank discussions with your parents so that together you can come up with acceptable ways of meeting their needs as they change. Preparing for the future in this way will make you feel less stressed out and will ensure that your parents maintain their sense of independence and dignity.

Talking about the situation

➤ Make a list: Consider giving your parent a list of questions or issues you would like to talk about so that he can prepare for the conversation and think about the kinds of help he may need.

➤ Reassure your parent that you have her best interest at heart and that you will handle any problems that come up together.

➤ Respect your parent's independence: Allow your parent to take an active role in the decision-making process. He will feel more in control if the meeting is in his own home. Just because your parent needs your help doesn't mean he is a child. Be careful to never talk down to your parent.

➤ Review legal, financial and medical matters that affect your parent so that you can make educated decisions.

➤ Have reasonable expectations about what your parent can do independently and be sure to consider her views.

> Voice your concerns: Be honest with your parent about limitations you may have—whether it's about handling your work while caring for young and old, or whether it's the financial costs to your family. Being responsible for your parent's care will require time, energy, and perhaps even some of your own savings.

> Get help from other members of your family—your spouse, siblings, aunts and uncles and even your older children. Have regular discussions with your family and anyone else involved in your parent's life and care, and decide together who is responsible for which tasks or aspects of your parent's life. Good communication and general agreement (it's okay if you don't agree on every little detail) among all concerned will help everyone better handle a crisis.

> Deal with resistance: There is bound to be some discomfort in discussing your parent's need for help, so be gentle. You may want to involve someone whom your parent respects and feels comfortable with.

> Maintain a dialogue: If your parent needs care on an ongoing basis, you will need to have discussions regularly. You may think a particular issue has been addressed or a decision has been made, but it may take your parent a little longer to digest certain information and come to terms with the change. Check in with your parent or elderly relative to find out if he has lingering questions or is feeling uneasy about something. Really listening is the hardest part of caregiving (especially if what you are hearing are complaints), but it's also the greatest demonstration of your love.

Putting the issues on the table

Quality of life—your parent's and your own—is the most important factor in making decisions about your parent's care. Keep in mind how the decisions you make affect the lifestyles of everyone involved. Ideally, your parent should make her own choices, even if you don't always agree with them. She may be slowing down, but she still has goals and dreams. And while she should hold onto these, she may need to be persuaded to let go of other things, like a living situation that is no longer working or that is putting her health and life at risk.

It is rare for an aging parent to rush toward change with open arms. Your parent may be adamant about staying put, but if you are worried about him most of the time or if your efforts to care for him are wiping you out and robbing you of your family time, you need to let your parent know that it is not possible to "leave well enough alone."

If you need to make a major change in your parent's living situation, consider options that offer plenty of social contact. As people get older and friends and loved ones die, it is easy to feel lonely or isolated. And if you are going to have a lot of responsibility for your parent, you and your parent will both benefit from the support of friends and other family members. Your parent needs to maintain contact with friends and family other than you, and you will need regular access to friends or professionals that you can talk to freely about the frustrating aspects of your role as caregiver. You are likely to have conflicted feelings and this might make you feel guilty. That's why it's so important that you find places or groups you can go to and share your feelings without being judged.

Assessing the kind of help your parent will need

You will need to spend an extended period of time with your parent to really know how she is doing and figure out what her needs are. A 3-hour visit—or even a 24-hour visit—may not be enough. You will probably need to ask questions of people who live nearby or have regular contact with her. You will particularly want to monitor your parent's activities that pose safety risks, such as driving. You also need to find out whether your parent is eating properly, maintaining her appearance, and keeping her commitments—social and financial. Your parent might not like this, and might even accuse you of "spying" or talking about her behind her back. Explain calmly that her ability to take care of these necessities will help you both determine what kind of daily help she needs. Remind her that you are asking these questions because you love her and want her to be safe.

There are community resources that can help your parent remain independent and engaged, such as Meals on Wheels or programs that send volunteers to a parent's house to read aloud. Look online or make a few calls to find out what is available and how to sign up for the services that seem most promising.

What to Look Out For

These are some of the signs that it is time to have your parent live elsewhere, with someone, or to find at-home care or support services for him or her:

> Your parent stops taking his medication correctly (skips doses or takes the wrong dose). This can happen because he doesn't understand the doctor's instructions or because he is becoming forgetful and is not acting like himself.

> Your parent starts losing a lot of weight. She may not be eating enough or has lost interest in preparing foods.

> Your parent seems to be having accidents a lot or you notice that he always has bruises and burns. Medication, alcohol or forgetfulness could be behind this, or he doesn't have the strength he needs to get around his house and kitchen safely.

> Your parent no longer bathes or keeps up appearances. She may be unable or uninterested in grooming, or she may be unaware that her hygiene has slipped.

> Your parent has had several accidents or close calls while driving, or you feel uncomfortable being in a car with him when he is behind the wheel.

> Your parent is not keeping up with bills, friends or appointments.

> Your parent doesn't know the time of day or basic information that she used to rely on daily, or she doesn't recognize family members or remember their names.

▶

> ➤ Your parent seems uncharacteristically angry, disoriented or begins to behave strangely—heading out to a job he retired from long ago or is dressed for a day at the beach when there is snow on the ground.

Figuring out where your parent will live

One of the first things you have to think about is where your parent will live once she needs help. A parent's health and medical care requirements are a big factor in the decision. Does she need assistance with everyday living? Is moving in with you an option? What about a retirement community or assisted-living facility? Wherever your parents live, they may need safety handles in the bathroom or a lift for the stairs.

You should consider housing options before a crisis arises, because housing decisions may take months to resolve.

If you invite a parent to move in with you, be realistic about what would be required in having your parent in your home and how it would affect your family. While this living situation might put a strain on the family at first, multigenerational living—children, parents and grandparents all under one roof—are common in some countries and can bring families closer together.

When you live far from your parent

If you live far away, you will have to rely on others—neighbors, family, clergy, or health care professionals—to care for your parent and keep you informed. Be sure to introduce yourself to neighbors and friends and keep their phone numbers and addresses handy. You may want to consider consulting a geriatric care manager. This professional is trained in dealing with the needs of older people and will assess your parent's various needs and create a care plan—from housing to social services (visit *http://caremanager.findlocation.com*). A brochure describing housing options and the various levels of care available to older people can be found at this government Web site: *http://www.eldercare. gov/Eldercare/Public/resources/fact_sheets/pdfs/Housing%20Options% 20Booklet.pdf*

Some of the better facilities have waiting lists, so it is a good idea to plan in advance.

If a parent moves in with you

Sometimes, having a parent move in will be the best solution. Of course, if your parent is used to living independently in their own home, living under someone else's roof can be a big adjustment. The new living arrangement will pose changes and challenges for your family, too.

Agree on the rules. Establish the "house rules" up front so there are no surprises. Set reasonable boundaries and be willing to compromise where possible to accommodate your parent. For example, if your parent slept with the TV on at his house, but in your house the noise keeps people awake, you will need to discuss the problem and find a solution. Maybe you can ask your parent to turn off the television at a certain time or you could buy him some wireless earphones (one of your children might love setting this up and teaching his grandfather how to use the earphones!). Discuss any feelings or concerns your parent, spouse, or children may have and be willing to address problems openly.

Budget. Caring for a parent at home can take a financial toll on you. You'll need to establish a budget and determine what financial resources, such as Social Security or pension funds, your parent will be able to contribute. It may feel uncomfortable, but it is important to discuss finances before your parent moves in.

Encourage activities. You should encourage your parent to stay active and even help with household chores if he or she is physically able to. This will contribute to feelings of self-worth and usefulness, which is very important to a parent who has lost her independence. Let your parent know which chores you could use some help with, and find activities and classes that might be of interest. Maybe your mother has always wanted to take a drawing or quilting class, or learn to use the computer, and now she finally has the time to do it.

Give it time. Be patient. It can take a while for everyone to get used to the new living arrangements. Once the family is accustomed to the new routine, it can feel natural and enjoyable to have everyone together in the same house, all pitching in to help one another. Kids who share living space with grandparents are learning valuable lessons about the cycle of life—some of which they may put to use when you get older! We learn by being with people who are different, and older people have a different take on the world. If they force us to slow down, dress a little better, or watch our manners, this can be a wonderful thing.

Accept your limitations. If certain aspects of your parent's personality or your relationship bothered you before, those personality quirks can drive you to distraction when you are sharing a roof again. There are bound to be rough days. Just as you sometimes have to settle for being "a good enough mother" (or father), learn to live with being a "good enough child."

Help beyond housing

Legal issues. Make sure your parent's will and other legal documents are in order. An advance health care directive is important because it specifies what should be done to preserve his health or life in the event that your parent is no longer able to make decisions. If your parent becomes incapacitated or too ill to say what procedures he is willing to undergo or whether he wants his organs donated, you and his doctors won't have to guess what his wishes would be because they will be clearly laid out in writing. Many states have developed their own standardized form. You can look online or call the Eldercare Locator at 1-800-677-1116. For additional information on this and other legal matters, consult an attorney that handles wills, estates and elder care matters or a senior service organization in your community.

Financial issues. It is very important that you spend some time understanding your parent's financial situation. What is her income, how much does she have in savings or investments, and what are her regular expenses? Find out where bank statements and other financial documents are kept. Is your parent's health or long-term care insurance up-to-date? Is she eligible for Social Security or Medicare (Medicare provides medical coverage for most individuals over 65)? Even if your mother never held a paying job, she is probably entitled to Social Security if she was married for at least 10 years to someone who was employed. You should determine her short-term and long-term financial needs and resources and consult an accountant or other financial advisors. For information on additional financial assistance such as Medicaid, that might be available to your parent, go to: *http://www.ssa.gov/disabilityresearch/wi/1619b.htm.*

Health issues. Speak with your parent's primary physician about his physical, emotional, and mental functioning and any suggested treatment. Get a clear idea of your parent's limitations and strengths. Find out what medications your parent is taking and what side effects they may have. Some medications, for instance, can cause disorientation, confusion, and loss of physical agility. So before you panic and assume your father or mother has Alzheimer's, check to make sure your parent's condition isn't the result of a bad reaction to medicine.

Lori had a couple of emotional but productive talks with her dad. She was able to make him understand that his insistence on "staying put" and "not being a bother to anyone" was actually putting a great strain on Lori and her family. Even her job performance was suffering. She let him know how much he means to her but she also told him, "I can't do this alone. I am going to need help from a lot of people, including you!" They decided to rent out part of his house and use the income to help pay for in-home care. They have also made plans to visit some assisted living facilities and nursing homes near Lori's house so that if things change, they'll have a back-up plan. Now that Dad has regular help, Lori is able to concentrate on organizing his financial documents and doing the things only she can do for him. Lori still feels pulled in a lot of directions, but at least she's getting more sleep. Yesterday she even went for a walk with her daughter to get ice cream and just talk—something they hadn't had a chance to do since her dad's fall.

Additional Information/Resources

> The Eldercare Locator (1-800-677-1116) can tell you which local agencies provide services in your community. You can also visit *www.eldercare.gov.*

> Check the yellow pages or online for your Area Agency on Aging for information on free homecare and other services for people over 60. You can also go to the Web site of the National Association of Area Agencies on Aging at *www.n4a.org* to get links or phone numbers for the Agency on Aging in your state.

> For referrals on assisted living, visit the Assisted Living Federation of America's Web site at *http://www.alfa.org/custom/directory/.*

> AARP offers a big selection of valuable information for caretakers at *http://www.aarp.org/families/caregiving/caring_parents/.*

> Resources for caregivers developed by the Administration on Aging can be found at: *http://www.aoa.gov/prof/aoaprog/ caregiver/caregiver.aspx.*

Useful Books

> American Medical Association Guide to Home Caregiving by American Medical Association

> The 36-Hour Day: A Family Guide to Caring for People with Alzheimer Disease, Other Dementias, and Memory Loss in Later Life by Nancy L. Mace and Peter V. Rabins

Chapter Thirteen

The Single Parent:
Riding a Bicycle Built for Two...Alone

As a single mother, Denise thought things would get easier as her children got older, but now that they are in middle school, she's finding it harder than ever to keep up with her job and take good care of the kids. She rushes home each day as early as she can to help them with their homework, fix some dinner, and try to get them to bed at a decent hour. When Denise finally gets into bed and sets her alarm, she tries to ignore the fact that she's going to have to do it all over again in 7 hours. She feels like there isn't any give—there's no extra time or money and she's ready to snap. All it takes for her to lose her temper is to come home and find dishes in the sink (again) or to discover, after the kids have brushed their teeth, that her son has forgotten to do his math homework.

Being "single" is a word that many people associate with fun, but for the nearly 13 million households[1] with only one parent, "single" means you are the one responsible for everything. While there are many rewards (and you get to take most of the credit when things go well!), being a single mother or father is a challenging role.

In many cases, single parents have to be the breadwinner, cook, chauffeur, tutor, rule maker and enforcer, loving role model, and sometimes the playmate. It's difficult, maybe even impossible, to perform well at so many different jobs—especially day in and day out. A lot of single parents complain that the hardest part is transitioning from one job to the next: from the 9 to 5 one that pays the bills to the labor of love that is your home and family. During the day, you are someone's employee but when you come home you have to be boss—a steady and strong one who's a teacher, not a tyrant. If you lose your temper and end up screaming at your kids, they are bound to worry, *who's in control if you're losing control?*

Peddling hard

Raising kids alone is a little bit like riding a bicycle built for two—all by yourself. It's heavy, hard to steer, and you are doing all the peddling. And then there is that empty seat right in front of you or behind you, reminding you of what your children might be missing.

About one-third of kids in the U.S. live with only one parent (usually a mother), and the good news is that most of those children are doing just as well in school as kids with two parents.[2] The children of mothers who don't have much education and can't get or keep a job are likely to have problems—with or without a father. Single parents who don't fit this profile may be stressed out, but their children stand as good a chance as anyone's of turning out fine and even excelling.

How are those single moms holding up, and what can they do to make their lives a little easier?

If you are a single, working parent, you are going to have to peddle hard, but below is a roadmap to guide you and help you avoid some of the steepest hills.

Steer clear of bumps in the road

The number one hurdle for any single parent is managing the family's finances—bringing in enough money (with or without alimony and child support) to cover costs and save for the future. This is tougher for single mothers than single fathers because men and women still do not earn the same money for the same jobs (women earn about 77 cents for every dollar earned by a man).[3] A good resource for single mothers who want some financial guidance is the Web site, *www.wife.org* (the Women's Institute for Financial Education).

For single parents who are not struggling to pay the bills and who can put aside some money for a rainy day and their children's education, there are other issues, such as finding enough time and energy to give to your children, and coping with being a mother and father to your child when you yourself may need some nurturing.

Parents who are working long days and are unable to spend as much time with their children as they would like may worry that they are not being a "good parent." Some parents also worry that, if they are not available to supervise their children, their kids will get into bad habits or trouble after school. Guilt and worry can cause parents to buy too many gifts, say "yes" to too many questionable activities, and to fill up their kids' day with too many structured activities.

While finding and scheduling safe, predictable things for a child to do after school is a good idea, you don't want to end up with a child who is as overscheduled as you are. Too many commitments mean not enough down time or time to help *you* keep the household running smoothly. Just because you are out of milk, doesn't mean Mom has to go get it! If there is a store nearby, perhaps your child can help with those kinds of chores. Or, you could make your child responsible for telling you in advance when you're running low on milk, bread, peanut butter, or other essentials. One of the benefits of growing up in a single-parent household is that children are often entrusted with more responsibility and become, as a result, more responsible.

Too much of a good thing vs. enough good times

Avoid using presents as substitutes for your presence. Over-indulging does no one in the family any good—not your child, not you, and not your pocketbook. The child whose divorced parents are trying to outdo each other in terms of giving and allowing is doubly spoiled. And, this child soon learns how to play the two parents off each other to gain even more material rewards. None of us wants to send our kids the message that they are what they own. Instead teach them that they are what they *do*, and remember, they will be looking to you to set the example.

Try to make up for your absence or non-attendance at school games and plays in other ways—like devoting time on a weekend to doing things together that you and your kids enjoy. The "make-up" activities don't have to cost anything to be fun. Maybe you want to make brownies together (you can use a mix to make it easy, or make it from scratch to make it more of a project). Or, perhaps you've been meaning to organize your photos. Work on this once a month with your children. Not only will you enjoy re-living the memories captured in the photos, you will spend time together and have an album (on your bookcase or online) to share with visitors once the project is done.

Parents do not equal friends

When you do manage to spend time together, fight the urge to turn your child into your best buddy or BFF. Your child will be *in* your life for a long time, but as long as she is in school and dependant on you she is not your friend. A parent-child relationship is very different from friendship. You should treat your child with respect and your child should respect the fact that you are the one in charge. Try not to confide in your child or speak to her about personal matters that do not concern her or that might call for greater maturity. Even a child who seems mature may not be mature enough to hear about your relationships, whether friends, families, or lovers. Remember that long after you have forgotten what you confided, or forgiven the person involved, your children may still remember the time someone hurt your feelings—and they may hold that grudge forever because they are so loyal to you.

Coasting: learning to enjoy the ride

All parents—but especially single parents—should bone up on the 3 Rs of Home Life: Rules, Routines and Rituals. The 3 Rs are crucial to your sanity and your family's well-being.

When you are the only adult in the house and you have to work long hours, you depend on a certain amount of flexibility. It's the only way to fit everything in. You and your household have to learn to adapt and "go with the flow." It's a relief for parents to know that a sitter will come and they can work extra hours if need be, or that they can sleep late on a Saturday after staying up to meet a deadline. But avoid the temptation to become too informal—a quick bowl of cereal for dinner—or bend the rules too often. Your kids are counting on you to set an example. If everything in your life is an exception that you ask family members to allow "just this once" (over and over), your kids will expect to get away with the same thing. Stretch things too far or play too "loosey-goosey" at home and your family will lose its shape. And all of you will suffer from the lack of structure.

Children and teenagers need rules and predictability. They need to feel that some things—like pancakes on Sunday or Thanksgiving with their grandparents—are written in stone and are as immovable as a mountain. When your kids do test the limits, they don't *really* want you to give in: they want to feel you push back. Don't be fooled by their repeated requests, or even by their misbehavior.

Routines, like having dinner together several times a week or going on a family walk every Saturday, help cement the family bond. Rituals are the things we do to create a mood and mark a moment or day as special. They sustain us in times of difficulty and remind us of the importance of giving thanks and celebrating. If rules give a child boundaries and protect him, routines and rituals are what carry his safely through the days and years, deepening his love of life and family.

Tips for Single Working Parents:

Build in transition time. It's not easy to go from a work environment where you may need to rush to get everything done, to your home where being together and enjoying each other is as important as getting things done. While it's okay to be results-oriented, home life is often more about "process"—getting your child to open up about what is really bothering her or instilling the practice of homework in your son, rather than doing it for him. After all, if you make a great meal but you and your children are furious at each other while eating it, you have defeated the purpose of making that meal. Likewise, if your children get their homework done on time because you are telling them many of the answers, they aren't learning what they need to learn and you are teaching them bad habits. If you already passed 3rd grade, why are you doing your third grader's homework?

The transition from the office to home will be easier if you can relax by listening to music or books on tape in the car, bus or train; or by taking a relaxing 5-minute walk, or meditating *before* you take over at home. Or you can develop your own personal "back from the office" ritual that involves ten minutes of downtime when you first get home.

Make schedules, calendars and lists. Rules, routines and rituals help children become the people we want them to be, but schedules, calendars and lists are what help working parents juggle their dual responsibilities. Keeping yourself organized can keep you from losing your mind, and your cool.

Reach out. As a single, working parent you have to get to know your community—the resources and the people in it who can help you. Churches and community centers often offer after-care, "parents-night-out" babysitting, summer camps and other activities that can be very useful to single, working parents. But don't just rely on your neighborhood or these readymade networks. You also can create your own community, made up of people with needs and interests similar to yours. Visit the Web site *www.singleparentsmeetup.com* or *www.parentswithoutpartner.org*

▶

to find other single parents in your area. Another way to reach out is to form a single parents group within your children's school. You can all get together—adults and kids—for meals on the weekends or some evenings and share insights, babysitting references, and whatever else. And don't forget volunteer work. If you volunteer as a family on weekends or in the evening, you will expand your network of people with whom you trade favors and can count on in an emergency. Volunteering is a fun and meaningful way to spend time together as a family and can help build friendships with others.

Find substitutes when needed. Teachers have substitutes, workers are sometimes replaced with temps—wouldn't it be great if parents could have people to substitute for them when they can't be two places at once? There may be times when you want a family member or close friend to fill in for you when your work prevents you from attending a school play or soccer game. And if your child's other parent is not very involved in your child's life, you may want to enlist a relative or long-time friend to be available to your child as a second role model.

Your child may benefit from this other person's strengths and way of thinking, and may like knowing there is someone else to turn to—especially if he's a teenager and is having problems with you! Some single moms like this "understudy" to be someone who can set a positive male role model. It's a tall order to work full-time and play both mother and father to your children. Asking for help is not a sign of weakness; it is a way to enrich your child's life. Just be sure that this role model is someone you know well and trust completely.

Look for family friendly work. Flex-time, working from home, and job-sharing arrangements can all be good work options for a single parent. Even a regular 40-hour work week at the office can be easier if the boss is understanding and allows you to work from home occasionally. Get the job-training you need and keep your resume updated so that when better, more family friendly work opportunities arise, you can seize them. It's never easy balancing work and family, but having the right job can make a world of difference.

The me shift. There's the work shift, the family shift and the "me shift." See chapter 11, "Finding Time for Yourself (and Your Special

▶

Other) in a Hectic World," for ideas on how you can make sure to get a little time each day for you: for your hobbies, for furthering your career, for unwinding. Some single parents do this by staying up after the kids have gone to bed; others prefer to wake up early and have the house to themselves while everyone else is sleeping. That only works if you are still getting 8 or more hours of sleep each night (see Chapter 3, "Rise and Shine: Getting Enough Sleep"), which many parents find hard to do. Lunch hours and weekends are other opportunities to punch the "me clock."

Denise laid down some rules with her kids. She won't start dinner if there are dirty dishes in the sink, and kids who forget to do their homework still need to go to bed at the regular time but have to wake up early the next morning to get it done. Since her kids don't like getting up earlier, she's noticed they are forgetting assignments less often. Plus, she's losing her temper less frequently now that there are firm rules. Denise joined a single parents group that she found through the Internet. She's gotten a lot of ideas from other group members and she's even swapped childcare duties with another family she met through the group. She's still busier than she'd like, but the time she spends with her kids each day is much more enjoyable, and she's less tense at work, too.

Chapter

Fourteen

Plan B: What to Do in an Emergency or When Things Don't Go as Planned

Tricia doesn't want to be one of those moms who is always worrying about bad things that could happen. Even so, she knows that families need to be prepared for when things don't go according to plan. She doesn't like making important decisions at the last minute but sometimes, like when a child gets sick or hurt, she has no choice.

When a child is unexpectedly too sick to go to daycare or school, working parents don't have many choices. Usually, one parent wants to or has to take time off from work to care for that child. But there are days when, for one reason or another, neither parent is able to stay home. That is why it is important to have back-up—people or places you can turn to for help in these situations.

Who's covering home?

In a household with two parents, a sick child can sometimes be cared for by the parent with less work pressure or the one who can more easily work from home. Another solution is for the parents to share the sick day responsibilities—a tag team approach where each adult spends part of the regular work day at work and some time at home. When these options don't work out, parents have to look for alternatives.

If you have a regular babysitter who is not always available during the day or at the last minute, make a list of people who might be willing and available to stay with a sick child when your schedule doesn't allow you to.

The least costly and easiest choice is usually a family member or a retired neighbor or friend. A stay-at-home parent whose kids are going to be at school for most of the day might be interested in earning a little extra income, or might be willing to do you a favor if you will return the favor when he needs your help. This parent could watch your child, either at your home or at his or her home. And don't rule out local college students or high school grads who live with their parents in your neighborhood. Whether students or young employees, they may have schedules that involve many hours of free time during the day. After finding a back-up babysitter whom you like and trust, ask him or her for the names of several friends who would be interested in babysitting.

While more expensive, a very reliable option is to hire a licensed health aide through a home healthcare agency. Most of these agencies specialize in care for the elderly or care for very sick children who have to use medical equipment, but there are also companies that can send out babysitters with some health training on short notice. Visit *www.inhomecare.com* to find out if there are people in your area available to provide same-day sick-child care. You can also visit sites like *www.care.com* or *www.babysitters.com* to look for caregivers in your area who have experience with sick children. You pay more for care providers from agencies because they send out people who have no police record, who are bonded and insured, and who may have first aid training. The fact that they are bonded and insured means that if something goes wrong, the company will take responsibility and even pay damages. Some of these agencies have nurses on staff with whom the in-home care provider can consult if he or she has questions. The drawback to these services is you often have to pre-register for them and you can expect to pay $15 per hour and up.

Most daycare centers do not accept sick children, but some set up special sections or "sick bays" to accommodate families with illness. Sick-child daycare is so much in demand that some hospitals have established special programs, and there are even stand-alone centers and family daycare homes that exclusively deal with sick children.

Daycare centers that specialize in sick children are different from regular daycare centers because they have more highly trained staff, higher ratios of staff to children, and are tougher on hygiene and practices that can prevent the spread of illnesses. Just as in-home health care is more expensive than hiring a babysitter, sick-child daycare is more expensive than regular daycare. The good news is that more and more companies are offering to help cover the costs of emergency or sick child care. Some employers are even contracting with companies that provide in-home health care to ensure that their employees are never without the backup they need.

Bring your (sick) child to work day...or leave her at home alone?

If no one is available to care for your child and you can't afford sick child care or it isn't available in your area, you will have to improvise—something working parents are often very good at. If your child is not miserably or dangerously sick and your boss is open to the idea, you might consider bringing your child to work. Pack a blankie, food, and whatever else your child needs to stay busy. Just make sure your child doesn't disrupt work or sneeze on any of your co-workers, especially not the guy in the next cubicle who gets sick just from hearing someone cough.

Some states have laws specifying how old a child must be to stay home without adult supervision. If your child is old enough, you may decide for her to stay home alone. But, if so, make sure she knows what to do to stay safe. Your child must know how to call 911 and provide essential information like your home address and phone number. Instruct her on how to take her temperature and medications, and how to prepare the foods you would like her to eat. Also, go over with her basic rules like keeping the doors locked, never answering the door (unless it is a pre-arranged visitor), and not revealing to people on the telephone that she is home alone.

Home alone

A child's age is not the only factor in deciding whether he or she can be left alone. Maybe your child is able to take care of himself but he gets scared being home alone or is very nervous about it. Children mature at different rates, and a sick child may feel more vulnerable and less able to make good decisions or follow advice. The unforeseen inevitably happens, so the best way to be prepared is to have your child enroll in a first aid or safety course geared toward children. Visit *www.redcross.org/services/hss* and click on the link that says "your local chapter" to find out what classes are available near you. You and your children will feel much better about fall-back plans, like having a sick child stay at home alone, if they have been trained in basic safety.

Teach your children how to escape from the house in the event of a fire or other emergency, and how to reach you and other family members or friends. All important phone numbers should be posted next to the main phone. Let your child know you will be checking in frequently—at agreed upon times but also randomly when your work schedule permits it.

And of course, if a child is supposed to be at home, she needs to let you know if she is leaving the house. Calling and having no one answer is very unsettling for a parent, but particularly if the child is supposed to be in bed, sick.

Deciding if Your Child is Ready to be Alone

Below are some Web sites you can look at, recommended by the government[1], that will help you determine if your child is ready to be left alone and provide you with tips to keep your child safe:

American Academy of Child and Adolescent Psychiatry Home Alone Children (Facts for Families No. 46)
http://www.aacap.org/cs/root/facts_for_families/home_alone_children

KidsHealth (The Nemours Foundation's Center for Children's Health Media) — Leaving Your Child Home Alone
www.kidshealth.org/parent/firstaid_safe/home/home_alone.html

National Child Care Information Center — Children Home Alone and Babysitter Age Guidelines
www2.nccic.org/poptopics/homealone.html

National Network for Child Care — Home Alone
www.nncc.org/SACC/sac31_home.alone.html

Prevent Child Abuse America — "Home Alone" Child Tips
www.preventchildabuse.org/publications/parents/downloads/home_alone.pdf

---

What to do in a health emergency

Life happens, and that includes sudden and serious illness as well as accidents. When your adrenaline starts pumping and your mom or dad instincts kick in, it can be hard to slow down enough to think and evaluate the level of response needed for a particular emergency. Early and swift intervention can make all the difference—the difference between life and death—but overreacting can also cause you to waste precious time and money. This is what is so tough about being a parent: you have to seem all-knowing when you aren't (if you appear scared, how will your child feel?) and you must remain calm and composed enough to make decisions that may be difficult, even under less trying circumstances.

You will be much less likely to panic during an emergency if you have taken a pediatric first aid course and a course in cardiopulmonary resuscitation (CPR). These courses teach you how to stop bleeding, what to do if someone is choking, and what to do if someone has stopped breathing. Most courses are inexpensive, available through the Red Cross and other organizations, and are usually offered many times throughout the year. To find classes near you, you can use Google or another search engine on your computer, and type in "CPR class" and the name of your city or town. Courses are also available online, which means you can study and learn when it is convenient for you.

A course will help you better understand what a true emergency is and how quickly you have to respond. Illnesses and injuries fall into three broad categories:

> those that can wait until a doctor's visit,

> those that require same-day attention to avoid prolonged pain or a worsening of the condition, and

> those that require immediate action because they are life threatening.

This last type—true medical emergencies—usually require calling an ambulance or making a trip to the Emergency Room (ER) of a hospital. Emergency care is available 24/7, but the quality of that care varies. Not all ambulances or emergency rooms have staff trained to treat children, nor do they always have respirators or other medical equipment that are specifically designed for children. This is why it is important to ask your children's doctor, in advance, which emergency room is best, and which urgent care facility he or she prefers.

When to call an ambulance

If your child is unconscious, appears not to be breathing, has suffered a severe burn, or has a seizure lasting more than five minutes, you will need to call 911 for an ambulance. If he is so short of breath he can't speak or is turning blue (if this is due to choking, put your first aid course to use!), you will need an ambulance right away. If you suspect that your child has a head or neck injury, you should call an ambulance, because you could make the injury worse by trying to move him.

If your child has eaten, drunk or been exposed to poison, call the Poison Control Center at 1-800-222-1222 and find out if you need to call an ambulance.

Call for an ambulance if your child has been in a car accident or other accident likely to cause internal or excessive bleeding, or if your child is so injured or sick that she needs medical attention on the way to the hospital.

When to visit an urgent care center or the emergency room (ER)

Very few sicknesses and injuries require an ambulance. What is much more likely to happen at some point is that your child will need prompt medical attention when your doctor's office is closed—like in the middle of the night or on a weekend. You will then have to choose between an urgent care center and an emergency room or emergency department at an area hospital.

If the injury or illness is not life-threatening, urgent care centers can be a better and less expensive choice than the ER at your local hospital. Some centers specialize in pediatric care which means your child can get the medical attention he needs without the long wait at the ER. ERs have to serve everyone, ranging from victims of car accidents or fires to people with the flu who don't have health insurance and don't know where else to go. That makes ERs very inefficient, and is why a visit to the ER can take many hours and cost a lot.

Find out ahead of time about urgent care centers near you, the range of conditions they are equipped to handle, and which health insurance they accept. Your doctor should be able to recommend some urgent care centers that have board-certified specialists.

Many of them will schedule appointments on short notice, which can cut down on time spent in the waiting room. Urgent care centers can typically take x-rays, handle broken bones and sprains, give stitches, deal with allergic reactions, treat infections, and test for illnesses like strep throat. If you live close to a children's hospital, check to see if it has a room or division for urgent (not emergency) care.

Post the addresses and phone numbers of the urgent care centers in your kitchen or near the main telephone.

You Should Go to the ER if:

➤ You are unable to stop your child's bleeding (head wounds bleed the most).

➤ Your child is breathing with difficulty or has shortness of breath, is unusually sleepy or hard to wake up.

➤ Your child is having an asthma attack.

➤ Your child has slurred speech or she suddenly seems confused and can't make sense of things.

➤ Your child has a stiff neck together with a fever.

➤ Your child's heart is beating very fast without having done any exercise or his breaths are very quick and shallow.

➤ Your child has just eaten or drunk something poisonous or taken too much medicine (again, get advice from the poisoning help hotline: 1-800-222-1222. It operates 24 hours a day, seven days a week).

➤ Your child is under three months old and has a fever of 100.4 or higher, according to a rectal thermometer. You can call your doctor first, but if you are unable to get immediate advice, it is better to play it safe and head to the ER.

Tricia no longer thinks that preparing for the worst is like inviting something bad to happen. Instead of making her more worried, anticipating and planning for emergencies is helping her feel calmer and more in control. She has started a list of back-up babysitters and is collecting addresses and phone numbers of places to go in a medical emergency. Her next project is to make index cards for each child that will include their doctor's name, the names and doses of the medications they are taking, their allergies, major illnesses they have had, and whether or not they have ever been hospitalized and for what. In an emergency, whoever is home with the kids can just grab the cards and go.

Chapter

Fifteen

Help for the Holidays

T'was the holiday season and all through the store,
My wallet was empty, but still I bought more.
And dinner with family was just such a mess.
Oh, holiday time can be so full of stress.

As if working moms aren't busy enough

Holidays may be filled with glitter and joy, but the period between Thanksgiving and New Year's Day can also be a very chaotic, stressful time. The following tips will help you navigate the holiday whirlwind and keep you off the "naughty" list.

Watch your spending

With all the emphasis on shopping for the holidays, it may be hard to stick to your budget or resist the shiny, new toys that come onto the market at this time. To guard yourself against excessive spending, remember that the spirit of giving has to do with showing people you care, not showering everyone with expensive gifts. First ask yourself, "What bills need to be paid?" and "How much can I afford to spend this year on gifts?"

It is important to know how much money you will need to pay your monthly household bills and any credit card debt *before* you begin buying gifts. Put that amount aside or pay those bills early so that you won't end up overspending for the holidays.

Charging holiday purchases to your credit card is very convenient, but if you already have debt on those cards, or won't be able to pay your entire next bill, the $20 bargain you buy now could easily end up costing you more than $50 by the time it's paid for.

Think before you shop

Don't go into a store (or online) without knowing what you want to buy. You will save time and money by being prepared before you see the many sale signs. Create a list of gift ideas and figure out exactly who you will buy gifts for and how much you can afford to spend on each gift. If you're not sure what you want to buy, at least be sure of who you will buy for and what you can afford to spend. Keep the list in your wallet, stick with your plan, and stay within your budget for each gift. And if you spend too much on one gift, that doesn't mean you should forget your budget for all the rest of the gifts you need to buy.

Tips for Shopping Safely:

> Use a credit card for all of your purchases online. Credit cards protect you under the Fair Credit Billing Act. Under this law, you won't be responsible for more than $50 for disputed charges on credit cards and you have the right to withhold payment while a disputed charge is investigated. If merchandise that is delivered is defective, you have the right to send it back to the merchant and not pay for it. It is much more difficult to get your money back when you've paid by a check or cash.

> Print out copies of all of your online transactions and keep them. This paper trail should include product descriptions, the price you paid, copies of emails between you and the online seller, and most importantly, the online receipt. According to the Federal Mail or Telephone Order Merchandise Rule, whatever you order online should be delivered within 30 days unless the seller has told you otherwise.

> When heading to the shops, only bring the credit cards and identification that you are going to need. Remember, the more you bring with you, the more you can lose or have stolen. Leave your social security card and any other information someone might use to steal your identity at home.

> This is the time of year to be extra cautious when shopping— keep money well hidden, which means don't count it at the cash machine or linger there after making a withdrawal. Charges to your credit card should be processed within sight—not off in a backroom somewhere. Be sure to put away change and cards after each purchase and don't carry too many packages at a time as this makes it difficult to keep track of and hold onto your purse or wallet.

> If you store packages in the car, make sure they aren't visible. Park in a safe, well-lit place and write down where it is—it's easy to get confused.

Eat, drink, and be merry

The holiday season gives us a little extra liberty to eat the things that we may stay away from the rest of the year. Enjoy yourself, but in moderation.

People at a healthy weight add about a pound during the holidays and generally take it off in the spring, provided they are physically active. Unfortunately, most adults in the U.S. are already overweight, and overweight adults tend to gain more during the holidays and are less likely to lose it.[1] A "few extra pounds" can really add up, year after year! Research shows that most people eat when food is in front of them, even if they aren't hungry. So, eating before a party probably won't help you avoid temptation. That's also why it is better not to stand or sit next to the food at parties. Remember that eggnog and alcoholic beverages add a lot of calories. And alcohol reduces your inhibitions, making food all the more enticing.

Research also shows that people eat and drink more when their plates and glasses are larger, so whether you are a guest or a host, try using smaller glasses and smaller dishes to keep eating and drinking—and calories—under control.

Family and friends

For many of us, the key to enjoying family and friends is moderation. Don't overstay your welcome or let others overstay theirs. Avoid the topics that tend to create tension, and if you need help (whether from your spouse, children, or others), ask for it rather than expecting it to be offered. That includes help with keeping guests' children under control, help with preparing or serving food, clean up, or any other kind of help. When people are busy or having a good time, they don't always realize that their assistance is needed or expected.

Yours, mine, and ours

Divorced and blended families face particular challenges at holiday time. Combining family traditions, juggling conflicting schedules, staying on top of custody logistics, and making the children feel at ease with the changes in their lives are some of the hurdles blended families face. Here's how to make your holiday season merry.

Blending families

Forge new traditions. There is nothing wrong with bringing established family traditions to your step family, but also consider creating new rituals that lend a unique identity and bring a feeling of togetherness to your new family. Your children can work together to make a seasonal display using items found in nature (pine cones, dried gourds, etc.) or make holiday ornaments. Come up with your own holiday menu, with everyone suggesting and even contributing a favorite dish. Go on a special walk that you only do when you are together—in the woods, along a river, or to an area where you can take in holiday displays. Find songs you all enjoy singing or make some up. Another wonderful way to be together is to pick a cause you believe in and volunteer as a family.

Keep it simple. Go easy on yourself by reducing the flurry of holiday events. You do not need to have a Martha Stewart celebration. Try spreading out the holidays with mini-celebrations instead of getting together only on the major festivity days.

Plan ahead. Communicating your plans with your ex-husband, extended family, and others involved in your holiday will reduce the unexpected. Whenever possible, involve your children in holiday planning. This will give them a sense of involvement and importance.

Keep your cool. Emotions can run high during the holidays. For the sake of your children, try to rise above any conflicts. Your kids will be relieved to see the adults in their lives getting along and acting... like adults. Your children may feel torn between you and your "Ex" during the holidays. If they're visiting with their other parent, banish their guilt and encourage them to have a good time.

Encourage kids to express their feelings. Remember that changes in families can be rough on all the children involved. Reassure them that confusing or conflicting emotions are natural, and encourage them to talk about their concerns.

Take care of you. It is important for parents to make time for themselves. Although it's difficult to "be good" at holiday time, eating right, exercising, and getting enough sleep will reduce stress and keep you energized.

Holiday Do's and Don'ts for Parents who are Divorced or Blending Families

Be flexible with custody arrangements. Shared custody over the holidays is one of the most common problems for children of divorce. Children should not be put in the position of feeling torn between their parents. Confirm the arrangements well in advance and share the schedule with your children. Be willing to compromise where needed to reduce conflict.

Don't overspend on gifts. Divorced parents often compensate for feelings of guilt with extravagant gifts. Remember, it's the love behind the gift that counts. You don't have to break the bank to show you care. You should also explain to children that people have different incomes and ways of giving.

Keep the tone upbeat. When talking to your children, frame the changes they are experiencing through the merging of families in a positive light. Instead of focusing on loss, emphasize the addition of loved ones and new traditions to their lives.

Single for the holidays

Spending the holidays without a significant other can bring on the blues at holiday time. The absence of a partner while watching other couples enjoy the holidays can be extremely difficult. The holidays also add new demands to the already-packed schedule of a single, working parent. You can beat the blues by:

Spending time with friends. Alone for the holidays? Don't be! If you will not be with your family, plan to spend time with friends, particularly other single parents. Spending time with people you enjoy can go a long way in lifting your spirits.

Helping others. There's no better way to get your mind off of your own problems than to help someone else. Consider volunteer work such as feeding the homeless. In addition to the joy of lending a hand, it is an opportunity to meet other volunteers.

Seeking professional counseling. The loss of a spouse through divorce or death can bring on a sense of depression and grief that may be worse during the holidays. These feelings are very common and are often helped by talking to a therapist. The following government Web site provides helpful advice for picking the kind of counselor that is right for you. It also gives phone numbers and Web sites of organizations that can refer you to counselors in your area: (*http://mentalhealth. samhsa.gov/publications/allpubs/KEN98-0046/default.asp*)

The children are nestled all snug in their beds,
Visions of a great holiday dance in their heads.
You kept to your budget and still it was fun,
Juggling parties and relatives, and now it's all done!

REFERENCES

Reducing Stress for a Healthier You and a Healthier Family

[1] Kiecolt-Glaser JK, Toovey, E, McDonald A. Slowing of wound healing by psychological stress. *Lancet* 1995; 346:1194–1196.

[2] Kiecolt-Glaser, JK, Loving TJ, Stowell JR, Malarkey WB, Lemeshow S, Dickinson SL, Glaser R. Hostile Marital Interactions, Proinflammatory Cytokine Production, and Wound Healing *Arch Gen Psychiatry*, 2005; 62:1377–1384.

[3] Taylor, S. E., Klein, L.C., Lewis, B. P., Gruenewald, T. L., Gurung, R. A. R., & Updegraff, J. "Biobehaviorial Responses to Stress: Tend and Befriend, Not Fight or Flight" *Psychol Rev*, 2000, 107(3):41-429. *http://www.findem.com.au/resources/tendandbefriend.pdf*.

Geary DC, Flinn MV. "Sex differences in behavioral and hormonal response to social threat: commentary on Taylor et al." *Psychol Rev*, 2002; 109;745–50; Discussion 751–3.

[4] Maciejewski, PK Prigerson HG and Mazure CM. Sex differences in event-related risk for major depression. *Psychological Medicine*, 2001; 31: 593–604.

Rise and Shine: Getting Enough Sleep

[1] "Americans today get less sleep and feel worse, study shows." *http://findarticles.com/p/articles/mi_m1355/is_n20_v90/ai_18743102*

[2] "Kids 5 and Under Sleep Less than Recommended Amount of Time, USA." *http://www.medicalnewstoday.com/articles/34388.php*

[3] "Sleep and Childhood Injury" *www.sleepfoundation.org/site/c.huIXKjM0IxF/b.2419315/ k.686C/Sleep_and_Childhood_Injury.htm*

[4] "Lack of Sleep Among New School-goers Leads to Behavioral Cognitive Problems." *http://www.sciencedaily.com/releases/2007/09/070901073630.htm*

[5] "Reduced Sleep Hurts Children's Academic Performance" by Katrina Woznicki. *http://www.medpagetoday.com/PrimaryCare/SleepDisorders/tb/2111*

[6] "Babies Lack of Sleep boosts later obesity risk." *http://www.cnn.com/2008/HEALTH/conditions/04/07/infant.sleep.obesity.ap/index.html*

[7] "The Impact of Moderate Sleep Loss on Neurophysiologic Signals during Working-Memory Task Performance" by Michael E. Smith, PhD, Linda K. McEvoy, PhD, and Alan Gevins, D.Sc

San Francisco Brain Research Institute and SAM Technology, San Francisco, California. In Sleep. 2002 November 1; 25(7): 784–794. *http://www.pubmedcentral.nih.gov/articlerender.fcgi?artid=1626388*

[8] M A Hack et al, "Comparison of the effects of sleep deprivation, alcohol and obstructive sleep apnea (OSA) on simulated steering performance," Respiratory Medicine 95 (July 2001) 594–601.

J T Arnedt et al, "How do prolonged wakefulness and alcohol compare in the decrements they produce on a simulated driving task?" Accident Analysis & Prevention 33 (May 2001) 337–344.

R Smith-Coggins et al, Rotating shiftwork schedules: Can we enhance physician adaptation to night shifts?" Academic Emergency Medicine 4 (October 1997) 951–961.

J J Pilcher, A S Walters, "How sleep deprivation affects psychological variables related to college students' cognitive performance," Journal of American College Health 46 (November 1997) 121–126.

[9] "Neurobehavioral Performance of Residents After Heavy Night Call vs After Alcohol Ingestion" J. Todd Arnedt, PhD; Judith Owens, MD, MPH; Megan Crouch, BA; Jessica Stahl, BA; Mary A. Carskadon, PhD. JAMA. 2005;294:1025-1033.

[10] Van Dongen, H.P., Maislin, G., Mullington, J.M., Dinges, D.F. The cumulative cost of additional wakefulness: dose-response effects on neurobehavioral functions and sleep physiology from chronic sleep restriction and total sleep deprivation. Sleep. 2003 Mar 15; 26(2):117-26.

[11] Spiegel K, Leproult R, Van Cauter E. Impact of a sleep debt on metabolic and endocrine function. The Lancet, 354: 1435–1439, 1999.

[12] Short Sleep Duration in Infancy and Risk of Childhood Overweight. Elsie M. Taveras, MD, MPH; Sheryl L. Rifas-Shiman, MPH; Emily Oken, MD, MPH; Erica P. Gunderson, PhD; Matthew W. Gillman, MD, SM. Arch Pediatr Adolesc Med. 2008;162(4):305–311.

[13] "Lack of sleep America's top health problem, doctors say."
http://www.cnn.com/HEALTH/9703/17/nfm/sleep.deprivation/#the
http://healthysleep.med.harvard.edu/healthy/matters/consequences/sleep-performance-and-public-safety

[14] "Sleep and Children's Health—Biological Factors That Affect Sleep, Societal Factors, Effects of Insufficient Sleep."
http://healthysleep.med.harvard.edu/healthy/matters/benefits-of-sleep/learning-memory

[15] http://education.stateuniversity.com/pages/2422/Sleep-Children-s-Physical-Health.html
Sleep and Children's Physical Health - Biological Factors That Affect Sleep, Societal Factors, Effects of Insufficient Sleep

[16] "Chronically Sleep Deprived? You Can't Make Up For Lost Sleep."
http://www.sciencedaily.com/releases/2007/07/070702145152.htm

Choosing the Right Child Care

[1] U.S. Department of Health and Human Services Administration, Maternal and Child Health Bureau. Child Health USA 2006. Rockville, Maryland: U.S. Department of Health and Human Services, 2006. http://mchb.hrsa.gov/chusa_06/popchar/0206wmcc.htm.

[2] American Psychological Association - *http://www.apa.org/pi/cyf/daycare.html*.

[3] *"Are There Long-Term Effects of Early Child Care?"* Jay Belsky, Deborah Lowe Vandell, Margaret Burchinal, K. Alison Clarke-Stewart, Kathleen McCartney, Margaret Tresch Owen, The NICHD Early Child Care Research Network. *Child Development* 78 (2), 681–701, March/April 2007.

[4] *"Effects of Child-Caregiver Ratio on the Interactions between Caregivers and Children in Child Care Centers: An Experimental Study"* by de Schipper EJ, Riksen-Walraven JM, and Geurts SAE (Radboud University Nijmegen, The Netherlands). Copyright 2006. The Society for Research in Child Development, Inc. *Child Development* 77 (4), July/August 2006. *http://www.medicalnewstoday.com/articles/47296.php*

[5] *http://www.census.gov/prod/2005pubs/p70-101.pdf*

How Can I Teach My Kids to Behave?

[1] *http://www.aap.org/healthychildren/08winter/HC-winter08-parenting.pdf*

Healthy Eating for Families

[1] Larson NI, Neumark-Sztainer D, Hannan PJ, Story M. "Family meals during adolescence are associated with higher diet quality and healthful meal patterns during young adulthood." Journal of the American Dietetic Association. 2007;107:1502-1510.

The National Center on Addiction and Substance Abuse (CASA) at Columbia University (2005). The Importance of Family Dinners II. New York. *http://www.casacolumbia.org/Absolutenm/articlefiles/380-2005_family_dinners_ii_final.pdf*.

Eisenberg et al. Family Meals and Substance Use: "Is There a Long-Term Protective Association?" *Journal of Adolescent Health*, 2008; 43 (2): 151 DOI: 10.1016/j.jadohealth. 2008.01.019

Eisenberg, Marla E., Neumark-Sztainer, Dianne, and Linda H. Bearinger. (2004). "Correlations Between Family Meals and Psychological Well-being Among Adolescents." *Archives of Pediatrics and Adolescent Medicine*, 158(8).

Videon, Tami M., and Manning, Carolyn, K. (2003). "Influences on Adolescent Eating Patterns: The Importance of Family Meals." *Journal of Adolescent Health*, 32:365–373.

[2] Shields M, Tremblay MS. Sedentary behaviour and obesity among Canadian adults. *Health Reports* (Statistics Canada, Catalogue 82-003) 2008; 19(2): 19–30.

[3] Television Watching and Soft Drink Consumption, Joyce Giammattei, Dr.P.H., GlenBlix, Dr.PH.. Helen Hopp Marshak, Ph.D. and colleagues *Archives of Pediatrics and Adolescent Medicine*, Vol. 157, September 2003, pgs. 882–886.

Kids, TV, and Video Games

[1] Schmidt ME, Pempek TA, Kirkorian HL, *et al*. The Effects of Background Television on the Toy Play Behavior of Very Young Children. *Child Dev* 2008; 79:1137–1151

[2] *http://www.kff.org/entmedia/upload/Zero-to-Six-Electronic-Media-in-the-Lives-of-Infants-Toddlers-and-Preschoolers-PDF.pdf*. 2003

[3] "Violent TV and video game exposure as risk factors for aggressive behavior among elementary school children." Paper by Douglas Gentile, Joe Eisenmann, David Walsh and Randi Callahan. Presented at XVII Biennial Meeting of the International Society for Research on Aggression in Minneapolis. *http://www.public.iastate.edu/~nscentral/news/06/jul/vtvvvgelem.shtml*

Buchanan AM, Gentile DA, Nelson, DA, Walsh DA, and Hensel J. "What Goes In Must Come Out: Children's Media Violence Consumption at Home and Aggressive Behaviors at School." Paper by Presented at the International Society for the Study of Behavioural Development Conference, Ottawa, Ontario, Canada (2002).

[4] American Academy of Pediatrics. *http://www.medem.com/medlb/article_detaillb.cfm?article_ID=ZZZNKWJGQ2D&sub_cat=17*

[5] "Video Games and Aggressive Thoughts, Feelings, and Behavior in the Laboratory and in Life," Craig A. Anderson, Ph.D., Iowa State University of Science and Technology and Karen E. Dill, Ph.D., Lenoir-Rhyne College, *Journal of Personality and Social Psychology*, 2000: 78; 772-90. *http://www.apa.org/journals/features/psp784772.pdf*

[6] "Associations between Media Viewing and Language Development in Children Under Age 2 Years." Frederick J. Zimmerman, Dimitri A. Christakis, Andrew N. Meltzoff *Journal of Pediatrics*, 2007: 151;364–368.

[7] Mendoz, JA; Zimmerman, FJ; Christakis, DA (2007) "Television viewing, computer use, obesity, and adiposity in US preschool children." *International Journal of Behavioral Nutrition & Physical Activity, 2007: 44*,1186–1479

[8] Hancox RJ, Milne BJ, Poulton R. (2004) "Association between child and adolescent television viewing and adult health: a longitudinal birth cohort study." *Lancet*, 2004: 364; 257–62.

Tips to Keeping You and Your Family Healthy

[1] "Birth Defects. Having a healthy pregnancy." The Centers for Disease Control, *http://www.cdc.gov/ncbddd/bd/abc.htm* (accessed on September 11, 2008)

[2] "25-Hydroxyvitamin D Levels and the Risk of Mortality in the General Population." Michal L. Melamed, MD, MHS; Erin D. Michos, MD, MHS; Wendy Post, MD, MS; Brad Astor, PhD. *Archives of Internal Medicine* 2008;168(15):1629–1637. "Reduced risk of physician-diagnosed asthma among children dwelling in a farming environment." William K. Midodzi, Brian H. Rowed, Carina M. Majaesic, and Ambikaipakan Senthilselvan. *Respirology* 2007;Volume 12 Issue 5, Pages 692–699.

[3] "Research hints that chicken soup remedy may have scientific validity in reducing cold symptoms." *http://www.unmc.edu/publicaffairs/chickensoup/newsrelease.htm* (accessed on September 11, 2008)

[4] "Antibiotic Resistance." American College of Physicians, *http://www.acponline.org/patients_families/diseases_conditions/antibiotic_resistance/* (accessed on August 20, 2008)

[5] "Expression of CD 14 and Toll-like receptor 2 in farmers' and non-farmers' children." Roger P. Lauener et al. Lancet 2002; 360: 465-466.

[6] "Home Treatment of Fever." American Academy of Pediatrics, *http://www.medem.com/medlb/article_detaillb.cfm?article_ID=ZZZXB1JODDC&sub_cat=0* (accessed on September 11, 2008)

Back to School: Getting Off on the Right Foot

[1] "Back to School Tips." American Academy of Pediatric News Release. *www.aap.org/advocacy/releases/augschool.cfm*

Kids and the Internet

[1] "David Finkelhor on net safety" in an interview conducted by Larry Magid of *SafeKids.com* on May 20, 2008. *http://www.connectsafely.org/articles--advice/safety-advice-articles/david-finkelhor-on-net-safety.html*

[2] "Raise parent's awareness of risks, benefits of cyberspace" by Deborah Johnson. February 2003. American Academy of Pediatrics News, the official news magazine of AAP. *http://www.aap.org/advocacy/JohnsonCyberspaceAware.htm*

Finding Time for Yourself (and Your Special Other) in a Hectic World

[1] Real Simple/GfK Roper Study as reported in "Make Time for Yourself" at *Realsimple.com* *http://www.realsimple.com/realsimple/package/0,21861,1734800-1815371-1,00.html* (Accessed August 21, 2008).

[2] Haviland, J. M., & Lelwica, M. (1987). The induced affect response: 10-week-old infants' responses to three emotion expressions. *Developmental Psychology, 23*(1), 97–104.

Lewis, M. (2000). The emergence of human emotions. In M. Lewis & J. M. Haviland-Jones (Eds.), *Handbook of Emotions* (2nd ed., pp. 265-280). New York: Guilford Press.

[3] "Meet the Life Hackers" by Clive Thompson. *The New York Times.* October 16, 2005. Accessed August 21, 2008, *http://www.nytimes.com/2005/10/16/magazine/16guru.html*

Caring for an Aging Parent

[1]   Charles R. Pierret. "The 'sandwich generation': women caring for parents and children. Monthly Labor Review. September 2006. http://www.bls.gov/opub/mlr/2006/09/art1full.pdf

[2]   "Prevention of Falls: Facts." American Academy of Orthopaedic Surgeons. http://orthoinfo.aaos.org/topic.cfm?topic=A00101 (accessed September 18, 2008)

[3]   "Effect of Physical Activity on Cognitive Function in Older Adults at Risk for Alzheimer Disease." Nicole T. Lautenschlager et al. Journal of the American Medical Association. September 3, 2008; 300:1027-1037. http://www.washingtonpost.com/wp-dyn/content/article/2008/09/02/AR2008090201818.html (accessed September 11, 2008)

[4]   "Folate and the methylentetrahydofolate reductase 677C—T mutation correlate with cognitive performance." (February 2006). Jane Durga, Martin P.J. van Boxtel, Evert G. Schouten, Michiel L.Bots, Frans J. Kok, Petra Verhoel. Nuerobiology Aging, Volume 27, Issue 2, 334-343. http://www.msnbc.msn.com/id/8294219/ (accessed September 12, 2008).

The Single Parent: Riding a Bicycle Built for Two...Alone

[1]   "Single-Parent Households Showed Little Variation Since 1994, Census Bureau Reports." March 27, 2007. U.S. Census Bureau News. www.census.gov/Press-Release/www/releases/archives/families_households/

[2]   "On Mother's Day, a hopeful finding for single mothers and their children from a Cornell researcher." Press release, May 6, 2004. http://www.news.cornell.edu/releases/May04/single.parents.ssl.html (accessed September 15, 2008).

[3]   "Facts for Features: Women's History Month, March 2006." (February 22, 2006). U.S. Census Bureau. http://www.census.gov/Press-Release/www/releases/archives/facts_for_features_special_editions/006232.html (accessed September 24, 2008)

Plan B: What to Do in an Emergency or When Things Don't Go as Planned

[1]   "Leaving Your Child Home Alone." Child Welfare Information Gateway. July 2007. U.S. Department of Health and Human Services, Administration for Children and Families, Administration on Children, Youth and Families, Children's Bureau, http://www.childwelfare.gov/pubs/factsheets/homealone.pdf

Help for the Holidays

[1]   NIH News Alert: "Holiday Weight Gain Slight But May Last A Lifetime." March 22, 2000. National Institutes of Health. http://www.nichd.nih.gov/news/releases/holidayweightgain.cfm

THE NATIONAL RESEARCH CENTER
FOR WOMEN & FAMILIES

The National Research Center for Women & Families is a nonprofit organization that is dedicated to improving the health and safety of women, children and families.

Families are bombarded with information that seems to be intended to help them, but sometimes the goal is not so much to inform as it is to sell a product or an idea. TV news and media sound bites don't always present information clearly and accurately. The Internet has a great deal of information, but not all of it is reliable. It's hard to know what to believe. The National Research Center for Women & Families cuts through the hype to provide a clear, unbiased explanation of new studies and information. The Center improves the lives of more than 50 million people each year by providing them with information they can use from a voice they can trust. See our Web site—www.center4research.org—for more information on a wide range of issues that are important to you, your friends, and family.

The National Research Center for Women & Families gathers, analyzes, and critiques scientific and health information, and then explains that information in everyday language that is unbiased and easy to understand. The Center shares its findings with the public, the media, opinion leaders, and policymakers in order to improve programs and policies and to educate and empower individuals to live healthier and happier lives, prevent illness and obtain the best possible medical treatments.

The Center's staff has been interviewed on all the major TV news media and by national newspapers such as *The New York Times*, *The Washington Post*, *The Washington Times*, *USA Today*, and *The Wall Street Journal*, as well as other important newspapers such as *The Los Angeles Times*, *The Chicago Tribune*, *The Miami Herald*, *The Philadelphia Inquirer*, *The Baltimore Sun*, *The Boston Globe*, *The New York Daily News*, and magazines such as *Newsweek*, *U.S. News & World Report*, *The New Yorker*, *Time*, *Glamour*, *Family Circle*, and *Self*, just to name a few.

ABOUT THE AUTHORS

Diana Zuckerman, Ph.D.

Diana Zuckerman, Ph.D. is the President of the National Research Center for Women & Families, a research and education charity that works to improve policies and programs that affect the health and safety of women, children and families.

Dr. Zuckerman received her Ph.D. in psychology from Ohio State University and was a post-doctoral fellow in epidemiology and public health at Yale Medical School. She started her career as a psychologist on the faculty of Vassar College and then directed research on the impact that television has on children as a faculty member at Yale University. After a post-doctoral fellowship focused on research on mental health and public health, she directed a groundbreaking research study of college students' life goals at Harvard University.

Since 1983, Dr. Zuckerman has worked to improve the health of adults and children across the country. She is the author of four books, numerous book chapters and dozens of articles in medical and academic journals and in newspapers across the country. She has been interviewed as a health and safety expert on all the major TV networks, including ABC, CBS, NBC, CNN, Fox News, and public television, as well as by *The Today Show*, *20/20*, *National Public Radio* and major U.S. print media such as *The New York Times*, *The Washington Post*, *The Washington Times*, *Los Angeles Times*, *USA Today*, *Chicago Tribune*, *Chicago Sun-Times*, *Boston Globe*, *Detroit Free Press*, *New York Daily News*, *Newsweek*, *Time*, *U.S. News & World Report*, *Family Circle*, *The New Yorker*, *Glamour Magazine*, *Self Magazine*, and many other newspapers, magazines and radio programs.

Dr. Zuckerman has been President of the National Research for Women & Families since 1999. She has also served on the faculty of George Washington University, guest lectured at American University, the University of California, and the University of Maryland, and is a Fellow at the University of Pennsylvania Center for Bioethics. She has served on numerous boards and commissions, and until recently was the chair of the Governor's Women's Health Promotion Council for the State of Maryland.

In addition to her expertise as a psychologist and expert on a wide range of health and mental health issues, Dr. Zuckerman knows what it is like to be a working mom. She is the proud mother of two children, ages 17 and 21, and worked throughout their childhood.

Brandel France de Bravo, M.P.H.

Brandel France de Bravo is the Director of Public Affairs and Communications at the National Research Center for Women & Families.

Ms. France de Bravo holds a Master's in Public Health from Columbia University and is a graduate of Warren Wilson's Master of Fine Arts Program for Writers. She is co-author of *Trees Make the Best Mobiles: Simple Ways to Raise Your Child in a Complex World* (St. Martin's Press), which has also been translated into Spanish and Japanese. Ms. France de Bravo has appeared on *The Today Show* and other TV and radio programs to discuss the challenges families face caring for small children. She has been giving parenting classes and workshops in Washington, D.C. for the last six years and has served on the Early Childhood faculty at the Washington Waldorf School. She is the happy mother (most days) of a 12-year-old girl.

Ms. France de Bravo's writing and editing skills have earned her prizes and fellowships, including a grant from the Washington D.C. Commission on the Arts and Humanities. Her book of poems, *Provenance*, was published in the fall of 2008.

In addition to being a writer and parent educator, Ms. France de Bravo has two decades of experience in international and U.S. health programs, primarily in HIV/AIDS prevention, reproductive health, and maternal and child health. As an expert in social marketing and behavior change, she has developed health education campaigns using a variety of media and has designed, conducted and analyzed quantitative and qualitative research. Prior to joining the National Research Center for Women & Families in 2008, Ms. France de Bravo consulted for such organizations as the United States Agency for International Development, the World Health Organization, the World Bank, the Open Society Institute and Population Services International.